CULTURES OF THE WORLD
Taiwan

Cavendish
Square

New York

Published in 2017 by Cavendish Square Publishing, LLC
243 5th Avenue, Suite 136, New York, NY 10016
Copyright © 2017 by Cavendish Square Publishing, LLC

Third Edition

Library of Congress Cataloging-in-Publication Data

Names: Moiz, Azra, 1963- author. | Wu, Janice, author. | Nevins, Debbie, author.
Title: Taiwan / Azra Moiz, Janice Wu and Debbie Nevins.
Description: New York : Cavendish Square Publishing, [2017] | Includes index.
Identifiers: LCCN 2016015897 (print) | LCCN 2016016022 (ebook) | ISBN 9781502618467 (library bound) | ISBN 9781502618474 (ebook)
Subjects: LCSH: Taiwan--Juvenile literature.
Classification: LCC DS799 .M65 2016 (print) | LCC DS799 (ebook) | DDC 951.249--dc23
LC record available at https://lccn.loc.gov/2016015897

Writers: Azra Moiz, Janice Wu; Debbie Nevins, third edition
Editorial Director, third edition: David McNamara
Editor, third edition: Debbie Nevins
Art Director, third edition: Jeffrey Talbot
Designer, third edition: Jessica Nevins
Production Assistant, third edition: Karol Szymczuk
Cover Picture Researcher: Jeffrey Talbot
Picture Researcher, third edition: Jessica Nevins

PRECEDING PAGE
Cherry blossoms bloom in the garden at the Tien Yuan Temple in Tamsui.

CONTENTS

TAIWAN TODAY

TAIWAN IS AN ISLAND ABOUT 112 MILES (180 KILOMETERS) OFF
the coast of China. It's one of the happier places on Earth—and definitely one
of the happiest in Asia. That assessment, by the World Happiness Report, is
based on a survey of 156 countries according to certain measurable indicators of
well being. In 2016, Taiwan ranked thirty-fifth, gaining three places over its previous
standing eighteen months earlier. In fact, Taiwan scored particularly well compared
to most of its neighbors in Asia, coming in well ahead of Hong Kong, Indonesia, Japan,
South Korea, and, interestingly, China—which ranked eighty-third.

All of this is not as frivolous as it might seem. Scored scientifically, the analyses
provide a surprisingly accurate portrait of a country's general quality of life, in
measures that reflect more than just national prosperity—though that is certainly
one factor. Some of the other happiness indicators include life expectancy, generosity,
the freedom to make life choices, social support, and perceptions of corruption in
society and government.

Taiwan's relative happiness, therefore, is an intriguing finding, considering its
unusual situation. For Taiwan is caught in position of indeterminate status—it is

A protester addresses the crowd at a large demonstration in Taipei against Taiwan's 2014 trade pact with China.

both a country called the Republic of China (ROC), and not a country; a sovereign nation and not a nation—depending on who or what makes the determination. Even if, for purposes of international expediency, Taiwan is considered a de facto country, it is still in an awkward position. The small island is a David to a huge and powerful Goliath—the People's Republic of China (PRC), which looms mightily over the island from across the Taiwan Strait. (In this analogy, no one expects this David to bring down Goliath; the best he can hope for is to hold off the giant, indefinitely.) The PRC, or mainland China, considers Taiwan to be its own renegade province—a pesky runaway that needs to be reunited with its true family. To that end, China refuses to have diplomatic relations with any nation that recognizes Taiwan (ROC) as a nation.

Given the enormous importance of China, this has forced most countries to reluctantly choose China over Taiwan. For this reason, Taiwan was booted out of the United Nations in 1971. Even the country's name is a matter of dispute. The PRC opposes the official name of Republic of China or even the name Taiwan because those names imply Taiwan's status as a sovereign state. It also insists there is only one China, not two. This name dispute causes problems even in supposedly nonpolitical realms, such as the Olympics. (Of course, the Olympic Games have long been a showcase for political frictions of all sorts.) For Taiwanese athletes to compete in Olympic events, the two Chinas agreed upon the deliberately ambiguous name Chinese Taipei as a designation for Taiwan.

This peculiar "betwixt and between" status affects the life of the Taiwanese in many ways. Their history as a people was enormously impacted by the cataclysmic revolution that took place in China in the mid-twentieth century. It was then that the government of China fled to the island and set up as a government in exile. That exile status became permanent as it became clear that the mainland communist government was there to stay. Today, Taiwan's political parties are mostly split between those who foresee eventual reunification with China and those who imagine independence. The economies of the two countries have become deeply connected, and even person-to-person ties are tightening as tourism flows in both directions.

In 2016, the Taiwanese elected Tsai Ing-wen as its new president, putting an end, for now, to the previous administration's trend toward deepening ties with China. Tsai, a member of the Democratic Progressive Party (DPP), took 56 percent of the vote to become Taiwan's first female president. She is opposed to reunification. "The people expect a government that can lead this country into the next generation, a government that is steadfast in protecting this country's sovereignty," she said after her victory. That doesn't mean she is looking to upset the apple cart by aggressively pushing back at China. "We will work towards maintaining the status quo for peace and stability across the Taiwan Strait in order to bring the greatest benefits to the Taiwanese people," Tsai told a press conference after her victory. "Both

Tsai Ing-wen holds a press conference after her election victory in January 2016.

A Taiwanese father and son pose happily for a photo.

sides of the strait have a responsibility to find mutually acceptable means of interaction."

Despite the expected rumblings and warnings from China, the status quo of ambiguity seems to be the best choice forward for now. Neither China nor Taiwan wants to aggravate tensions to a crisis point over the island's identity. However, one might expect that living with constant uncertainty of this sort would cause anxiety among the Taiwanese. That's why the results of the latest World Happiness Report are so interesting. The Taiwanese have obviously learned how to live in the unsettled situation they find themselves in, and apparently are not living in great fear of the future.

More concerning, according to a 2016 poll conducted by the Taipei City-based newspaper *United Daily News*, are high housing costs, pension reform, and taxation equity. Young Taiwanese, in particular, are distressed about growing social inequality and a widening wealth gap.

On the other hand, gender equality is improving in this traditionally patriarchal culture. The election of the first woman president is surely a sign of progress, and even before Tsai's victory, the Taiwanese government promoted and supported women's rights. The workplace gender gap is shrinking. In 2013, the country's female labor participation rate stood at 50.46 percent, the second year in a row that it rose above 50 percent. That year, women made up 33 percent of the ROC legislature—a rate that exceeded comparative numbers in Japan, South Korea or the United States.

Taiwan is a relatively small island, but it has achieved a degree of prosperity disproportionate to its size. In just four decades, it made the leap from being a poor agricultural society to being one of Asia's most dynamic industrial economies. Taiwan's economic success and its problematic political standing in the international arena have often overshadowed the island's natural beauty as well as its multifaceted culture. Nevertheless, while the island's natural landscape presents stunning and dramatic geographical vistas— jagged mountains in the central region contrast with the flat wide plains in the coastal regions—it is the people of Taiwan who bear within them the essence of the island's nature. These are the very people whose heritage and traditions have spanned the centuries and who, despite political difficulties, face the future with confidence and conviction.

The financial district of Taipei is dominated by the distinctively tall building Taipei 101.

GEOGRAPHY

A cow grazes on Penghu Island off the west coast of Taiwan.

GEOGRAPHICALLY SPEAKING, AT least, Taiwan is an island. That much is indisputable. Whether or not Taiwan is a nation is a whole other question. The people who live on the island call it the Republic of China and act as if it is an independent nation. The people who live on mainland China, or the People's Republic of China (PRC), Taiwan's huge neighbor 112 miles (180 km) to the west, vehemently disagree, but that's a discussion for a different chapter.

Compared with mainland China, Taiwan is quite small, with an area of 13,969 square miles (36,179 square km). This makes it slightly smaller than Switzerland or the Netherlands, or about the combined area of Connecticut, Massachusetts, and Rhode Island. The shape of the island has been likened to a leaf or a sweet potato—it is long and tapers at its southern end. At its broadest point, the island of Taiwan is 89 miles (144 km) wide; from north to south, it is 244 miles (394 km) long. China is Taiwan's closest neighbor to the west. Korea and Japan lie to the north and the Philippines to the south. The Tropic of Cancer, which runs across the Earth's surface at a latitude of 23.5°N, cuts across the island about midway.

The earliest Portuguese sailors who set foot on Taiwan were so impressed with the lush beauty of the country's dramatic mountains and lovely coastal scenery that they called it Ilha Formosa, meaning Beautiful Island. Part of this name stuck, and for centuries after this, Taiwan was widely known in the West as the island of Formosa.

The Republic of China consists mostly of Taiwan but it also has jurisdiction over small groups of scattered islands. These include the Penghu archipelago with its sixty-four islands off the western coast of Taiwan, Kinmen (Quemoy) and Matsu Islands, as well as twenty other islands, including Lü-tao (Green Island), Lanyu (Orchid Island), and Chimei. As Taiwan itself is an island, the seas are an important feature of its geography. The Taiwan Strait (or Formosa Strait) separates Taiwan from China to the west, and the Bashi Channel divides it from the Philippines to the south. To the north lies the East China Sea and to the east, the Pacific Ocean.

Taiwan is one of a chain of islands in the western Pacific. Over ten thousand years ago, during the last Ice Age when sea levels were lower, Taiwan may have been connected to the mainland by a land bridge. Today, any land bridge is submerged under the Taiwan Strait, but the fact that sea depths in the strait are relatively shallow, about 230 feet (70 m) deep, has been used to support the theory behind the land bridge. In contrast, off the east coast of Taiwan, in the Pacific Ocean, the sea depth plummets to thousands of feet.

GEOGRAPHICAL REGIONS

Taiwan has one of the most varied landscapes in Asia, all within short distances of each other—snowcapped mountains and subtropical bamboo forests, sandy beaches and white-water rapids, gentle green hills and deep rocky gorges. Almost two-thirds of the island is covered with the mountains of the Central Range, and the rest is made up of foothills, terraced tablelands or plateaus, coastal plains, and basins. About 90 percent of Taiwan's population is located in the more low-lying areas of the terraced tablelands and coastal plains. Because half the land is forested and almost 40 percent is used for agriculture and other purposes, approximately only 10 percent of it remains to house Taiwan's 23.4 million people and to accommodate its industries.

CENTRAL MOUNTAIN RANGE AND OTHER MOUNTAINS Believed to have been formed over one million years ago by the collision of the Earth's continental plates, the Central Mountain Range is Taiwan's most dominant physical feature. Stretching from Eluanbi in the south to Suaoin the north,

the long line of mountains rises gently in the west but plunges dramatically into the sea on the eastern coastline. More than sixty peaks in the Central Range soar above 10,000 feet (3,000 m). The highest mountain is Yü Shan (YOO-shahn), meaning Jade Mountain, in Yü Shan National Park.

Yü Shan is actually a large mountain mass made up of eleven peaks. Its main peak is the highest point in northeast Asia, standing at 12,965 feet (3,952 m). Along the eastern margin of the Central Range, the mountains rise steeply, creating spectacular scenery with deep gorges and valleys. A narrow coastal belt lies along the east coast where the mountains end. To the west, the incline of the mountains is more gradual as they slope down gently into foothills and plains.

For many years, the mountainous Central Range posed a natural barrier to traveling to the isolated eastern regions. In 1960 the East-West Cross-Island Highway was constructed at a cost of $11 million. Built to facilitate travel within Taiwan, the highway stretches from the western coastal plain to the east coast, curving 120 miles (193 km) across the Central Mountains. This highway has helped to open up the eastern region to farming, cattle raising, logging, and tourism.

Taiwan also has pockets of volcanic mountains. The Tatun Mountains, north of Taipei and near Chi-lung, are of volcanic origin. The presence of hot springs and fumaroles issuing hot gases shows that this northern region still has some geothermal activity. On the northeastern coast, some mountains

Yü Shan Mountain gleams like jade in some light, which accounts for its name, Jade Mountain.

of volcanic origin can also be found. Consequently, this area experiences frequent earthquakes and earth tremors.

FOOTHILLS AND TERRACED TABLELANDS

Around the mountains of the Central Range lie the foothills. Most of the foothills are on the western side of the range, and they have an average height of 4,000 to 5,000 feet (1,220—1,520 m). Terraced tablelands—sandstone gravel deposits accumulated from erosion—lie between the foothills and coastal plains, at elevations of 330 to 1,640 feet (100—500 m). The broadest tableland can be found in the region between T'ao-yüan County and Hsin-chu County in northern Taiwan.

COASTAL PLAINS AND BASINS Coastal plains run along the western coast from the north to the southern tip of the island. Their rich and fertile alluvial soil has supported waves of immigrants from the mainland for hundreds of years, earning them the appellation "the rice bowl of Taiwan." The flat terrain of the western coast contrasts with the rugged mountains of the Central Range. As the plains are well drained by rivers, they are the focus of agriculture and settlement. The largest is the Chianan plain in the southwest, which makes up 12 percent of Taiwan's land area. Taiwan's major urban centers are located in the coastal basins—the Taipei Basin in the north, T'ai-chung Basin in the central west, and P'ing-tung Basin in the south. Three major municipalities—Taipei, T'ai-chung, and Kao-hsiung—are also situated there. The western coastline is lined with tidal flats and swamps.

At the southernmost point in Taiwan stands the Eluanbi Lighthouse. It was built in 1882 atop the rugged coastline to warn ships of the presence of dangerous submerged coral reefs.

The Eluanbi Lighthouse, sometimes called "The Light of East Asia," faces the Luzon Strait at the southernmost tip of Taiwan.

RIVERS AND DRAINAGE

All of Taiwan's rivers rise in the mountains of the Central Range. The longest rivers are the Choshui at 116 miles (187 km) and the Kaoping at 106 miles (171 km). Although most of the rivers are not long, they drain a relatively large area. The Tan-shui, which flows northward toward Taipei, drains 1,052 square miles (2,725 sq km); the Choshui drains 1,218 square miles (3,155 sq km) of the western coastal plain; and the Kaoping drains 1,257 square miles (3,256 sq km) of the southern plain near Kao-hsiung. The Wu River is only 73 miles (119 km) long and yet drains 782 square miles (2,026 sq km). Many of Taiwan's rivers have been dammed to generate hydroelectricity.

ISLANDS OF TAIWAN

Known as the Pescadores (meaning Fishermen's Islands) by sixteenth-century Portuguese sailors, the Penghu archipelago is made up of sixty-four islands in the Taiwan Strait. Situated approximately midway between Taiwan and mainland China, it has a land area of 49 square miles (127 sq km). Only twenty islands in the archipelago are inhabited, and almost half the total population of the main island of Penghu lives in the main town of Ma-kung. Penghu is the only Taiwanese county that is also an archipelago. Linking Penghu to nearby Paisha and Hsiyu islands is the Penghu Great Bridge, or Trans-ocean Bridge—the longest inter-island bridge in the Far East. Built originally in 1970, the bridge was damaged by the weather and ocean tides, and was subsequently rebuilt and reopened to the public in 1996. It now spans the length of 8,182 feet (2,494 m).

The Kinmen (Quemoy) and Matsu islands are the Taiwanese islands closest to mainland China. Kinmen is 150 miles (240 km) from Taiwan Island and only 1.4 miles (2.3 km) from mainland China, while Matsu is about 1 mile (1.6 kilometers) from the mainland. The Kinmen islands, twelve islets lying off mainland China's Fujian Province, cover a total area of 58 square miles (150 sq km).

The Penghu Islands' natural harbors once served as safe havens for pirates who attacked the Chinese coast. Today, the islands are among the world's major sources of coral.

The main island in this group is the rocky and hilly Kinmen Island. The Matsu islands lie 131 miles (211 km) from northern Taiwan, off the northeast coast of Fujian Province. This island group has nineteen islets, the largest of which is Nankan. Being so close to mainland China, Kinmen and Matsu are mainly military outposts, although there does exist a small nonmilitary population inhabiting both islands that fishes and farms for a living. Kinmen is also the site of a national park.

Lanyu, or Orchid Island, is named after the profusion of wild orchids that grow on the island's hilly slopes. It has an area of 17 square miles (44 sq km). Lanyu is the home of the Yami aboriginal people, who make a living chiefly from fishing in the surrounding sea.

Taiwan's other islands include Chimei, also called the Island of Seven Beauties, south of Penghu; Hsiao Liuchiu, off southeastern Taiwan; and Lü-tao, or Green Island, off the eastern coast.

Besides these islands, Taiwan has also laid claim to two other groups of islands in the South China Sea—the Pratas and Spratly islands (called Tungsha and Nansha by the Taiwanese). The Spratly Islands are also claimed by five other Asian countries: China, Vietnam, the Philippines, Malaysia, and Brunei.

Orchid Island, off the coast of southeast Taiwan, is also the site of a nuclear waste storage facility, despite the opposition of the resident aboriginal Tao people.

CITIES

Close to 90 percent of the people in Taiwan live in urban centers.

TAIPEI Meaning "north Taiwan" in Mandarin, Taipei is the political, cultural, and economic center of Taiwan and its largest city. It is Taiwan's capital city and a special municipality that sits at the northern tip of the island. Taipei grew out of a settlement that was established in the latter half of the 1600s on the banks of the Tamsui River. Although it gradually developed in the centuries that followed, Taipei remained a provincial and relatively underdeveloped town; even as late as the 1950s, many rice and vegetable farms could be found within the city limits. Few now remain. The economic prosperity of the 1970s and 1980s saw the construction of many modern high-rise buildings. Present-day Taipei is a cosmopolitan city of 2.6 million people. However, adding the population of the surrounding area (New Taipei City, a municipality created in 2010) brings the total for the metropolitan area to about 6.9 million.

The Neihu District of Taipei gleams in contrast to the dark hills and mountains that surround it.

KAOHSIUNG In the southwest, facing the South China Sea, Kaohsiung is Taiwan's second largest city. It is an important shipping center and harbor, with a population of 2.7 million. Besides being Taiwan's biggest international seaport, Kaohsiung and its environs are also Taiwan's most important industrial areas, with heavy industries dealing in petrochemicals, cement, shipbuilding, steel, oil, and sugar refining. Recent trends, however, have shown that Taiwan's economy is becoming increasingly dependent on high-tech industries located mostly in the north.

TAICHUNG Taichung, which means "central Taiwan," is the country's third largest city, with nearly 2.7 million people. It is located midway along the North-South Highway that runs from Taipei to Kaohsiung and is an important industrial city, producing a wide range of manufactured goods. Taichung was founded in 1721 and was first called Tatun by settlers from mainland China. Since 1976 it has become an important seaport, with the development of a harbor west of the city.

TAINAN Tainan, the oldest city in Taiwan, served as the country's capital from 1684 to 1887. It is the fourth largest city in Taiwan today and is well known as a cultural and historic center.

CHIAYI The city of Chiayi lies on the western coastal plain. It is a small municipality that has some manufacturing industries. It functions mainly as a departure point for excursions to the Central Mountain Range.

CLIMATE

Because Taiwan is surrounded by warm ocean currents, it has a warm climate. The northern region tends to be cooler than the south, so it is often said that Taiwan's climate is subtropical in the north and tropical in the south. During the hot, humid summers that last from May to September, the temperature reaches 80 to 95 degrees Fahrenheit (27—34 degrees Celsius). December through February is wintertime, with mild temperatures of 54 to 61°F (12—16°C). Because the winters are very mild, snow hardly ever falls in Taiwan

TYPHOONS-TERROR FROM THE SEAS

Every July to September, Taiwan does battle with typhoons and tropical cyclones called tai fong *(TAI fohng). These typhoons are usually summertime phenomena, when strong, violent winds of up to 100 miles (161 km) per hour and driving rain sweep across the country. An average of three typhoons hit Taiwan every year, and the southern and eastern regions are usually the most badly affected.*

In August 2009, Typhoon Morakot caused more than six hundred casualties in Taiwan, making it the island's deadliest typhoon to date. Extraordinarily heavy rainfall—109.3 inches (2776 millimeters)—caused a mudslide that buried the entire village of Xiaolin, killing some five hundred residents there alone. In September 2015, a "super typhoon" Dujuan hit the island, killing two people and injuring more than three hundred. Wind gusts were as a high as 153 mph (246 km) and some areas received more than 35 inches (900mm) of rain in just one day, which is about one third the average annual rainfall for Taiwan. Dujuan came just weeks after Typhoon Soudelor killed six people on the island.

Typhoons have become so much a part of life in Taiwan that people automatically prepare for them. Taiwan's International Community Radio Taipei and Weather Control Bureau constantly monitor and advise the public on the status of typhoons by publishing condition alerts:

Condition 24: . . . . . . Typhoons may hit in twenty-four hours.
Condition 12: . . . . . . Typhoons may hit in twelve hours.
Condition 8: . . . . Typhoons may hit in eight hours.
Emergency Alert: . . . . Typhoons have hit the island.

During typhoon alerts the island comes to a standstill as people stay at home to ride out the storm. In homes, people prepare for floods and winds by packing up or securing loose items. Because electrical power can fail if power lines are knocked down, people stock up on batteries and candles. Extra drinking water and food are also stored in case of emergencies—even after a typhoon has blown itself out, there is still a real risk of landslides and floods.

SUN MOON LAKE

The largest and one of the most famous lakes in Taiwan is Sun Moon Lake. According to legend, it was once two separate lakes—Sun Lake and Moon Lake—but earth tremors caused the two lakes to merge together. Ever since then, it has been called Sun Moon Lake. At times, some turbulence and earth movements can still be felt in the lake, causing the water to shoot up as high as 20 feet (6 m) into the air.

Today it is part of Sun Moon Lake National Scenic Area, a popular recreation and tourist destination in Taiwan. It is also a source of hydroelectric power.

Indeed, Taiwan's geography continues to be reshaped in a similar fashion today. An earthquake on September 21, 1999, created a new lake in the central mountains and caused a slight rise in the altitudes of some mountain summits.

except in parts of the Central Mountains.

Taiwan's weather pattern is greatly affected by the monsoons. The northeast monsoon brings heavy winds and rain from the East China Sea from October through March. Usually the northeast region and the eastern coast are the most heavily affected, although people living on the west coast also have to take precautions. During the southwest monsoon from May to September, the situation is reversed so that southern Taiwan has wet weather and northern Taiwan is drier. Rainfall in Taiwan is high, at about 100 inches (254 cm) per year.

"Taipei's weather is like a stepmother's temper" is a common complaint by many of Taipei's residents, who have to put up with high humidity and constant rain. Because Taipei is ringed by mountains that trap moisture, summers are uncomfortably hot and humid; in winter, a light drizzle can persist for weeks on end.

FLORA AND FAUNA

Taiwan's flora, which is similar to that of mainland China, varies with the altitude. In lowland regions below 2,000 feet (610 m), palm and other evergreen trees are found. The most common tree is the acacia. Mangroves are abundant in tidal areas, and bamboo flourishes all over the island, especially in the areas that receive the highest rainfall. Cedars, maples, and cypresses can be found up to 7,000 feet (2,130 m), and coniferous alpine forests do well at the highest elevations. Forests cover 55 percent of the island, mostly in the Central Mountains.

Taiwan has abundant native and migratory bird life due to its strategic location. More than six hundred species of birds have been recorded on this island. There are also at least twenty-five bird species that live nowhere else but Taiwan. The country lies at the crossroads of a major migration route for birds and therefore is an important pit stop for hundreds of migratory birds.

Other animals found on the island include various kinds of deer; the Formosan macaque, Taiwan's only primate; and the hard-to-find Formosan black bear, its only bear. It is this rich diversity of wildlife that Taiwan's growing conservation movement aims to preserve.

The *Prunus mei*, or plum blossom, is the national flower of Taiwan. It has a delicate fragrance and comes in pastel shades of pink and white. The mei blossom is a hardy flower. Because it blooms in winter, it has come to symbolize perseverance and courage for the Taiwanese.

INTERNET LINKS

Intreasures.com/taiwan.html
This site lists Taiwan's unique plants and animals.

lifeoftaiwan.com/about-taiwan/geography-climate
This page offers a quick overview of Taiwan's geography and climate.

www.lonelyplanet.com/taiwan
This travel site has beautiful photos from many destinations in Taiwan.

HISTORY

The pagoda and pond at 2/28 Peace Memorial Park in Taipei commemorates the victims of the February 28 Incident of 1947.

2

HUMANS HAVE BEEN LIVING ON Taiwan for some twenty or thirty thousand years. More than one thousand archaeological sites of various prehistoric cultures dot the island, but yet little is known about these early settlers. More than ten thousand years ago, the bottom of the Taiwan Strait was exposed as a broad land bridge connecting Taiwan to mainland China, so it's likely people arrived that way. The land bridge has, of course, long since disappeared under rising seas. These primitive people, who left evidence of a Stone Age culture, died out mysteriously around five thousand years ago. Later waves of migrants and settlers, in particular the aboriginal people and the Han Chinese, left more lasting impacts on Taiwan.

In November 2015, Taiwan's President Ma Ying-jeou and China's President Xi Jinping held historic talks in Singapore. It was the first such face-to-face meeting between the two Chinese presidents since the end of the civil war, which split the nations in 1949.

THE ABORIGINAL SETTLERS

Early records from mainland China, dating from the third century CE, note the presence of aboriginal peoples living along the coast of Taiwan. Of Austronesian stock, the aborigines probably migrated to Taiwan from Southeast Asia. The early aboriginal people belonged to a number of groups and were mainly fishermen, hunters, and farmers. Apart from occasional intertribal warfare, they lived peacefully until their existence was disrupted by the arrival of the mainland Chinese in the thirteenth century.

EARLY CONTACTS WITH CHINA

Although Taiwan's history is often tied to that of mainland China, the early Chinese emperors considered Taiwan to be outside their sphere of influence. The earliest record of mainland China's contact with Taiwan dates back to 239 CE, when an expeditionary naval force was sent to explore Taiwan. From the seventh century onward, Chinese naval forces sent patrols to Taiwan to police the seas separating the island from the mainland. These were not attempts to assert control of Taiwan but actions to protect Chinese trading ships in the area from attacks by pirates.

The Formosan Aboriginal Culture Village theme park features the traditional architecture and boats of the native people.

During the Yuan Dynasty (1271—1368), Taiwan was a protectorate of the Mongol Empire by the Mongol emperor Kublai Khan (1215—1294). It was around this time that the first waves of Chinese immigrants began arriving in Taiwan. Coming mostly from the Fujian and Guangdong provinces in China, they first settled along Taiwan's western coastal plains. They were followed by another wave of immigrants from Fujian Province in the fourteenth and fifteenth centuries, during the Ming Dynasties (1368—1644). These and later waves of settlers caused severe disruption to the aborigines, who were either absorbed into the migrant populations, or forced to leave their villages in the plains and retreat to the mountains and the remote east coast. The

DYNASTIES OF CHINA

Throughout its four thousand years of history, mainland China has had a succession of ruling families, called dynasties. Taiwan's history has been closely associated with China since the time it was declared a Chinese protectorate during the Yuan Dynasty.

Xia Dynasty . . . . . . *21st–16th century* BCE	*Sui Dynasty* *581–618*
Shang . . . . *16th century–1066* BCE	*Tang* *618–907*
Zhou . . . . *1066–221* BCE	*The Five Dynasties* *907–960*
Qin . . . . *221–206* BCE	*Sung* *960–1127*
Han . . . . *206* BCE*–23* CE	*Yuan* *1271–1368*
The Three Kingdoms . *220–265* CE	*Ming* *1368–1644*
Jin *265–420*	*Qing* *1644–1911*
Southern Dynasty. . . *420–58*	*Republic of China.* *1912–1949*
Northern Dynasty. . . *386–581*	*People's Republic of China* *1949*

migrants claimed land from the aborigines and cultivated crops such as rice and sugarcane. As these settlers prospered, Taiwan, in turn, became an important trading area.

EUROPEAN ARRIVAL

In the sixteenth century, drawn by the prosperous trade of the region, the Portuguese, Spanish, and Dutch began to take an interest in Taiwan.

The Portuguese, the first to arrive in the 1500s, named the island Ilha Formosa. Then, in 1624, the Dutch invaded Taiwan and set up a trading post at T'ai-nan. They also built forts to reinforce their military strength. The most famous are Fort Zeelandia and Fort Provintia. Later, the Spanish landed on the northern part of Taiwan and set up a fortified commercial post at Chi-lung and later at Tan-shui. The Dutch seized the Spanish settlements and drove them out in 1641. In this way, the Dutch extended their influence from the initial southwestern region to the northern regions as well.

The Dutch remained the colonial masters of Taiwan for less than a quarter of a century until they were themselves expelled from Taiwan in 1662 by Cheng Cheng Kung (Koxinga), a loyal general of the Ming Dynasty.

KOXINGA

Meanwhile, the fall of the Ming Dynasty in mainland China prompted an influx of refugees into Taiwan in 1644. One of these refugees was Zheng Chenggong, better known as Koxinga.

A general and warlord in the Ming Dynasty, Zheng (1624—1662) remained loyal to the Ming emperor in the face of the dynasty's collapse and the rise of Manchu Qing power. In recognition of his loyalty and courage, the Ming emperor granted Zheng the honor of using the royal family's surname, and Zheng then became known as Guoxingye, or Koxinga, Lord of the Imperial Surname.

After resisting the Manchu advance for as long as he could, Koxinga finally retreated to Taiwan along with his remaining troops and warships.

A stone statue of Koxinga honors the seventeenth-century hero.

He planned to drive the Dutch out of Taiwan and set up a base from which to overthrow the Manchus. A year later, in 1662, the Dutch surrendered control of Fort Zeelandia, their last stronghold in Taiwan (Fort Provintia had earlier been seized by Koxinga). With the end of Dutch colonial occupation, Koxinga became the ruler of Taiwan.

Today in Taiwan, Koxinga is regarded as a national hero and a *junzi* (or *chun tzu*), meaning "perfect man." His son and grandson carried on the Cheng name as rulers of Taiwan until 1683, when Manchu forces from the mainland took control of the island. Taiwan became a prefecture of Fujian Province in 1684.

JAPANESE OCCUPATION

Taiwan remained under Manchu rule for the next 212 years, although the Chinese hold on the territory was nominal. Except for a brief period in 1884—1885, when the French occupied parts of northern Taiwan and the Penghu islands, Manchu reign was left relatively intact until 1895, when the Japanese occupied Taiwan. In 1894 the Sino-Japanese War broke out over a dispute about the status of Korea. China lost the war and in 1895 was forced to hand over control of Taiwan to Japan under the Treaty of Shimonoseki. This marked the beginning of the Japanese occupation of the island. Initially, the Taiwanese resisted the Japanese and declared their island a republic, but this insurgency was soon crushed.

Japanese rule lasted from 1895 to 1945 and brought about many changes to Taiwan. The new colonists set about improving the infrastructure of the country, building roads, railroads, schools, ports, and other facilities. This, in turn, improved Taiwan's economy. Agricultural schemes were promoted, and agricultural production boomed. As a result, Taiwan became a major exporter of rice and sugar. With the development of hydroelectric dams in 1903, industry was also given a boost. Coal mining, forestry, and iron and steel industries added to Taiwan's development during the fifty years it was under Japan's rule.

However, there was a negative side to the Japanese occupation of Taiwan. The Japanese tried to crush nationalist feelings among the population, usually with harsh methods. Pro-China sentiments were also suppressed, and use of the Chinese language was discouraged in favor of Japanese. Japanese became the language of instruction in schools, and all official and business correspondence was required to be conducted in Japanese. During World War II, many Taiwanese were forcibly conscripted into the Japanese army. The Japanese occupation came to an end with Japan's defeat in World War II. Taiwan was returned to China in 1945.

TURMOIL IN CHINA

While the Japanese occupied Taiwan, a great upheaval was taking place in China. In 1911, the last Manchu Qing emperor was deposed in a revolution led by Sun Yat-sen, and China became the Republic of China (ROC). When Sun found he could not gather widespread support for himself, he stepped aside for Yuan Shih-kai to become president of the republic. Yuan declared himself emperor in 1915 but died shortly after. China plunged into further turmoil, with the former warlords of the Qing Dynasty competing for control. For some years a state of civil war prevailed, although the Nationalists (the Kuomintang party, or KMT) led by Sun managed to regain control of the southern provinces by 1923.

In 1928 General Chiang Kai-shek of the GMD defeated the northern warlords and unified China. But China continued to be destabilized by a growing Communist movement. In 1931 Japan invaded Manchuria in northern China, and by 1937 had overrun China's eastern seaboard. From a base deep in China's western heartland, the ROC fought a war of resistance, receiving aid from the Western Allied nations after the outbreak of World War II. When Japan was defeated, all of its colonies and captured territories reverted back to their previous status. This meant that Taiwan, formerly part of the Qing Empire before 1895, came under the control of the Republic of China.

Even after Japan's defeat in the war, China continued to be plagued by political upheaval, this time due to a struggle for power between the Nationalists and the Communists. In 1949, the Nationalists were dealt the final blow when the Communists led by Mao Zedong captured power.

FEBRUARY 28 INCIDENT

One of the most tragic dates in Taiwanese history is February 28, 1947. On that day, an anti-government uprising in Taiwan led to the deaths of thousands of citizens by the new KMT-led Republic of China government.

At the end of World War II, Taiwan was returned to China after fifty years of Japanese rule. The Kuomintang Nationalist Party, led by Chiang Kai-shek, was still in control of Mainland China, and it took control of the island. Initially, the Chinese Nationalists confiscated, looted, and stole whatever they wanted from the Taiwanese, which naturally led to friction between the mainlanders and the natives. In February 1947, those tensions erupted in an incident in Tapei that triggered public protests against the government. The demonstrations were brutally put down by ROC Army in what became known as the February 28 Incident. It was the beginning of a period of martial law, called the "White Terror" by the Taiwanese, during which some thirty thousand people were killed. Many killings were random, while others targeted dissenters and suspected anti-KMT activists. Thousands more were imprisoned.

The 228 Memorial Shrine

For many years, it was taboo to openly criticize, or even mention, the February 28 massacre. It wasn't until 1987, after martial law was lifted and 1995, when the president of Taiwan issued a formal apology, that the country faced the issue head on. Today, February 28 is commemorated as Peace Memorial Day in Taiwan, but the incident continues to haunt the country. A report released in 2006, the Research Report on Responsibility for the 228 Massacre, concludes that Chiang Kai-shek bore the greatest portion of responsibility for the period of terror.

Mao established the People's Republic of China (PRC) as the new communist nation. General Chiang, the KMT, and a total of 1.5 million Nationalist sympathizers fled the Chinese mainland to take refuge in Taiwan.

Instances of harsh Japanese rule in Taiwan caused some bitterness and resentment among the Taiwanese. During the Japanese occupation, in some Taiwanese communities, when a person died, his or her casket was carried to the graveyard under a black umbrella so that the deceased person would not be buried under a Japanese sun. Nevertheless, many Taiwanese still regard the Japanese period as a progressive era in their history, particularly in comparison with later Chinese Nationalist rule.

INVASION THREATS FROM CHINA

After the KMT's retreat to Taiwan, it appeared the Communists would invade the island. However, the new Communist government was preoccupied with destroying Nationalist pockets on the mainland and postponed the invasion of Taiwan.

When the Korean War erupted in 1950, US President Harry S. Truman ordered the US Seventh Fleet to patrol the Taiwan Strait and protect Taiwan against attack from China. This act was vitally important at this dangerous time because it was the presence of such a military force that kept the Communists from invading Taiwan. Since that time, Taiwan has been treading a thin political line with China. With financial and military backing from the United States, Taiwan was able to keep China at bay in the 1950s and 1960s in spite of the Communists' continued threat to invade the island.

During those years, Taiwan maintained its international status as a member of the United Nations (UN). It also claimed to be the rightful government of China, arguing that the Communists had seized the country by force, whereas the ROC was an elected government. Many nations, including the United States, accepted and supported this claim. China, on the other hand, declared that it was the legitimate government of all China, including Taiwan. Then, in the 1970s, under President Richard Nixon, the United States began a policy that helped it to forge a more cordial relationship with the

SUN YAT-SEN *Revered by the Taiwanese as the founding father of the Republic of China, Sun Yat-sen, a medical doctor, made his greatest political contribution by overthrowing the weak and corrupt Qing Dynasty and introducing democratic ideals to China. Born in 1866 in China's Guangdong Province, Sun spent some years studying in Hawaii before returning to China and qualifying as a doctor in Hong Kong.*

He was very much aware of the corruption inherent in the imperial system. In 1894 he formed the Hsing-chung Hui (Revive China Society), which aimed to end imperial rule and introduce democratic government, but did not succeed. Sun then spent the next sixteen years in political exile. He tried on at least ten occasions to topple the imperial court, again without success. On October 10, 1911, his followers captured Hubei Province in an armed uprising. Eventually, other provinces and cities joined the Nationalists and declared independence from imperial rule. Sun was elected president and inaugurated on January 1, 1912. During this time he reorganized his supporters to form the Kuomintang (KMT), the Nationalist Party. Sun spent the remainder of his life fighting to unify China. He died in 1925 at the age of fifty-nine.

GENERAL CHIANG KAI-SHEK *Chiang was born in 1887 to a family with a business background. Like many other young men of his time, he went to Japan to attend a military academy. And, like other young men, he became an anti-imperialist. In 1905 he cut off his pigtail in defiance of the Manchus. At the time, the pigtail was regarded as a symbol of Manchu rule and oppression. In 1908 he joined Sun Yat-sen's revolutionary group. After the 1911 revolution he became a major figure in the Nationalist army.*

With the death of Sun Yat-sen, Chiang became one of the GMD party leaders and the commander of the National Revolutionary Army. In 1927 he married Soong Mei-ling, the sister of Sun Yat-sen's wife. A year later, he became the president of the Chinese Nationalist government. After World War II, Chiang continued his struggle against the Communists but lost the battle for the Chinese mainland. From 1949 onward, Chiang was the president of the Republic of China on Taiwan. Although he spoke often about his sacred mission of reunifying China, he was unable to fulfill his vision before he died in 1975.

CROSS-STRAIT RELATIONS

So fragile are the political affairs between China and Taiwan that even referring to the issue can lead to trouble. Terminology is important, and whatever term one side prefers, the other finds offensive. Certain descriptors, such as "China–Taiwan," "PRC–ROC," and "Mainland–Taiwan," are already tainted with political implications favoring one side or the other. The People's Republic of China, for example, refuses to acknowledge the name Republic of China because it insists that such a nation does not exist.

The neutral term "Cross–Strait relations" has emerged as an acceptable way to discuss the topic. The term refers to the Taiwan Strait in the west Pacific Ocean, which separates mainland China from the island of Taiwan.

People's Republic of China (PRC). The United States established diplomatic relations with the PRC in 1979, and as a condition required by China, severed its diplomatic relations with Taiwan.

TAIWAN'S POLITICAL STATUS

For the past five decades, Taiwan and mainland China have fought a diplomatic battle on the international stage, each not recognizing the status of the other. This division between the "two Chinas" has been a sensitive issue. Nevertheless, there has been no large-scale military conflict between the two, although there were incidents in the 1950s and 1960s when the Chinese bombed the Taiwanese islands of Matsu and Kinmen, and the Taiwanese shelled the mainland from these two islands. However, since 1968 the only instances of military antagonism between mainland China and Taiwan have come in the form of missile tests and military exercises. Nevertheless, the issue has been kept alive in propaganda campaigns in both mainland China and Taiwan.

With each side claiming to be "the real China," Taiwan's political status has often taken a beating. In 1971 the UN recognized the PRC as the government of China, costing Taiwan its seat in the UN. Since then, and especially as the United States and other nations are on increasingly cordial terms with mainland China, Taiwan has had to work hard to uphold its status in the international arena.

In 1991 Taiwan's president, Lee Teng-hui, declared that the Republic of China on Taiwan would no longer claim to be the government of mainland China. He conceded that the People's Republic of China exercised the powers of government in the mainland areas and announced that the Taiwanese government would no longer try to use force to restore its power over the mainland.

In 2008, China and Taiwan initiated a program for normalizing—somewhat—transportation, postal, and trade communications between them. Prior to the "Three Links" agreements, all such interactions had to go through an intermediary. Gradually, direct commercial flights, shipping, and mail were instituted. However, as of 2016, China limits Taiwan-bound visitors with a quota system, and Taiwan visitors to the mainland are not permitted complete freedom. Some Taiwanese worry that opening these directs routes with mainland China will encourage more Chinese interference in the island's business.

The outgoing Taiwan President Lee Teng-hui waves to the crowd as he leaves office in 2000.

UNIFICATION OR INDEPENDENCE?

Some Taiwanese think their nation should give up on the idea of unifying with the mainland. Instead, they believe Taiwan should become completely independent from China. Many advocates of Taiwanese independence believe a declaration of independence is necessary or think that changing the country's name from "Republic of China" to "Republic of Taiwan" is a better idea.

An independent Taiwan is unacceptable to the People's Republic of China, which has promised to use force, if necessary, to prevent Taiwan from cutting its ties to China. Even though the two sides do not share a government today, supporters of unification believe they should do so in the future. A declaration of independence would make the establishment of a single

修改選罷法

補正公投法

ruling government much more difficult. The PRC government says Taiwan *is* a part of China, and that it should be ruled by the central government in Beijing. However, China's leaders say Taiwan could keep its own political and economic system. This formula is called "one country, two systems."

Most Taiwanese citizens are not eager for unification, and support for independence is growing, particularly among young people. These people tend to think of themselves as Taiwanese, not Chinese. A 2015 poll found that nearly 90 percent of the population in Taiwan would identify themselves as "Taiwanese" rather than "Chinese" if they had to choose between the two. Just 6 percent said they consider themselves Chinese.

That same poll found that a majority of people in Taiwan—65 percent—prefer to maintain the current political status, but that most—69 percent—would support independence if that or unification with China were the only two options.

2016 ELECTION

In 2016, Tsai Ing-wen became the first woman president of Taiwan, winning 56 percent of the vote. While she has pledged to maintain peace with China, and says she supports the status quo, Chinese officials on the mainland were wary. After Tsai's victory, the PRC's official Xinhua news agency quickly warned that Taiwan should abandon its "hallucination" of independence and that any move in that direction would be a "poison" that would cause Taiwan to perish.

President-elect Tsai Ing-wen cheers with her supporters at the Democratic Progressive Party headquarters in Tapei after her election victory on January 16, 2016.

INTERNET LINKS

www.bbc.com/news/world-asia-16178545
The BBC News provides a timeline of important dates in Taiwan's history.

www.forbes.com/sites/jnylander/2015/02/14/strong-support-for-independence-in-taiwan/#77d21dc26f8f
Taiwanese support for independence is the subject of this report.

www.lonelyplanet.com/taiwan/history
Lonely Planet offers a solid overview of Taiwan's history.

www.nytimes.com/2016/01/17/world/asia/taiwan-elections.html
This article reports on the election of Tsia Ing-wen as the first woman president of Taiwan.

GOVERNMENT

The Presidential Office Building is a famous historical landmark in downtown Taipei.

3

WHEN THE CONSTITUTION OF THE Republic of China was adopted in 1946, it was intended for the whole of China. The Nationalist Party, the KMT, still had official control of the mainland at that time. Taiwan has only just been returned to China from Japan a year earlier after the Japanese defeat in World War II. Civil war broke out almost immediately. When Mao Zedong's Communist forces defeated Chiang Kai-shek on the mainland in 1949, Chiang and the Nationalist ROC government fled to Taiwan. They brought the constitution with them.

Nevertheless, implementation of the constitution was put on hold as martial law was imposed. Elections for the legislature, presidency, and other political offices were suspended. Although critics argued that went against the democratic principles of the constitution, the KMT justified its policy on the grounds that it was necessary in the face of emergency conditions and the threat of invasion from the mainland.

In the 1970s, some Taiwanese citizens began agitating for the relaxation of these restrictions and for permission for more democratic practices. Democracy activists wrote books and magazines to publicize their ideas, took part in local elections and even won a few seats in

"The Republic of China, founded on the Three Principles of the People, shall be a democratic republic of the people, to be governed by the people, and for the people."
—Article 1 of the Constitution of the Republic of China, 1947

Taiwan election commission staff read out ballots as they count votes at a polling station in Taipei on January 16, 2016.

the ROC legislature. In what is now known as the Kaohsiung Incident of 1979, a group of activists clashed with the police during a demonstration, leading to the arrest and imprisonment of a number of democracy activists.

Forty years of martial law ended in 1987 when the KMT began to liberalize under the leadership of President Chiang Ching-kuo. Political parties were formed, and the democratic process envisioned by Sun Yat-sen came into being. In May 1991 President Lee Teng-hui announced the end of the Period of National Mobilization for Suppression of the Communist Rebellion. The first general elections to the Legislative *Yuan* (YOO-ahn), meaning council, and the National Assembly were held in December of that same year.

Taiwan's government is sectioned into central, municipal, and country-city levels. The yuan together with the office of the president make up the central government. The National Assembly, on the other hand, was a body whose functions were to ratify constitutional amendments and territorial changes to the public through referendums. It was abolished in 2005. Taiwan today has a national government with a president, five yuan, and twenty-five country and city governments. The most important government officials are the president, the premier, who heads the cabinet, and the legislators, who make the laws.

Voting age in Taiwan, as of 2016, is twenty, though many younger Taiwanese want to see it lowered to eighteen.

THE CONSTITUTION

Taiwan operates under the law of the Constitution of the Republic of China, which has been in effect since 1947. The constitution ensures the equality of all citizens before the law; freedom of speech, religion, residence, privacy of correspondence, and of assembly; the rights of existence, work, property, petition, election, and holding public office; the duties of paying taxes and performing military service; and the right and the duty of becoming educated, among other things.

THE THREE PRINCIPLES OF THE PEOPLE The three principles of the people form the basis of the constitution. They were formulated by Sun Yat-sen, who was influenced by democratic philosophies in Western countries, especially the United States, where he lived for some time. The principles are
- nationalism—independence for China, equality for all ethnic groups, and a sense of national identity in a common culture;
- democracy—political and civil liberties for each individual, and governing power to the organs of government; and
- social well-being—building a prosperous and just society where wealth is equitably distributed.

THE PRESIDENT

The president is the head of state and is directly elected by the people every four years. The first president of Taiwan was Chiang Kai-shek. During the years of martial law, when a state of emergency existed in Taiwan, the president was elected by the now-defunct National Assembly. After President Chiang Kai-shek's death in 1975, he was succeeded by his vice president, Yen Chia Kan. In 1978 Chiang Ching-kuo, son of Chiang Kai-shek, became president. In 1988 he was succeeded by Lee Teng-hui, the first native Taiwanese to become president.

In 1996 Taiwan held its first direct presidential election. At that time, the term was shortened from six years to four years. Lee Teng-hui was elected again, this time by the people of Taiwan. In 2016, Tsai Ing-wen became the first woman president of Taiwan.

FIVE BRANCHES OF NATIONAL GOVERNMENT

Most democratic countries have three branches of national government; Taiwan has five. The yuan are the executive, legislative, judicial, examination, and control.

EXECUTIVE The Executive Yuan functions as the national policy-making body, equivalent to a cabinet. It has a number of ministries, commissions, and councils, and is headed by a premier. The premier is appointed by the president and sanctioned by the Legislative Yuan.

LEGISLATIVE The Legislative Yuan is a single-chamber parliament and the highest lawmaking body. It is made up of 113 seats—seventy-three are elected in single member districts; thirty-four are elected based on the proportion of nationwide votes received by participating political parties, and six seats are reserved for aboriginal groups. Members serve four-year terms. After the National Assembly was abolished in 2005, most of its power and responsibilities, such as initiating constitutional amendments, were transferred to the Legislative Yuan.

JUDICIAL The Judicial Yuan is responsible for the legal system, which is composed of the Supreme Court, high courts, district courts, and administrative courts. The yuan's fifteen Justices of the Constitutional Court, or Council of Grand Justices, interpret the constitution and ensure that government action is carried out accordingly. Eight of the grand justices serve four-year terms, and the others serve eight-year terms. The Judicial Yuan also supervises the lower courts.

EXAMINATION The Examination Yuan is responsible for the examination, employment, and management of the civil service.

CONTROL The control yuan is a watchdog that audits or checks on the activities of the other branches of government and has the power to censure and impeach government officials.

POLITICAL PARTIES

From 1949 to 1987, when all political parties except the Kuomintang (KMT) were banned, Taiwan's government was effectively a one-party system.

The first sign of political liberalization came in 1986 when the Democratic Progressive Party (DPP) was formed. Since then, the political system has been increasingly democratized and liberalized into a competitive party system. With the ban on opposition parties lifted, over sixty political parties sprouted up in Taiwan. By 2014, there were 254 legally registered political parties in the ROC, but of course, most are minor parties.

There are two ideological blocs in Taiwan, commonly called the Pan-Blue Coalition and the Pan-Green Coalition. The Pan-Blues, led by the Kuomintang, favor the eventual unification with mainland China under the government of the ROC. Meanwhile, the Pan-Greens, led by the Democratic Progressive Party, tend to support eventual independence for Taiwan. Most members of both sides, however, say they prefer to maintain the status quo for now. Many minor parties in Taiwan are unaligned with either coalition.

Until 2000, the KMT had controlled the government for fifty-one years. In 2001 the DPP became the largest party in the Legislative Yuan, followed by the KMT. Other prominent political parties in Taiwan include the New Power Party and the People First Party.

INTERNET LINKS

www.cia.gov/library/publications/the-world-factbook/geos/tw.html
The CIA World Factbook gives up-to-date information on the government of Taiwan.

english.president.gov.tw/Default.aspx?tabid=1107
The Office of the President of Taiwan offers the text of the constitution in English.

www.taiwan.gov.tw
This is the official website of the Republic of China in English.

ECONOMY

Pedestrians walk down a bustling street in Taipei.

4

TAIWAN HAS A DYNAMIC CAPITALIST economy, the fifth-largest economy in Asia. From being a relatively poor country dependent on agriculture as its main source of income, Taiwan grew into one of the four "Asian Tigers"—the others were Singapore, South Korea, and Hong Kong—industrially developed, free-market Asian economies that maintained exceptionally high growth rates in the later part of the twentieth century. Taiwan was a newly industrialized economy that made the leap from manufacturing low-technology goods such as toys and clothes to manufacturing high-technology computers and aerospace systems.

Much of Taiwan's spectacular economic growth was due to an export-oriented strategy and the development of its infrastructure. In 1991, the government launched the Six-Year National Development Plan. A large-scale investment of over $300 billion in more than six hundred projects was planned for a number of sectors, including mass transit, the transportation industry, telecommunications, power generation,

"One thing we're concerned about is that as China grows, they want to recruit more people from key industries in Taiwan. To develop flat screens, LEDs, LCDs and solar power, they came and lured away people from Taiwan. Now we're worried that they want to develop integrated circuits, and to develop those they will take away a lot of people."
—Kao Shien-quey, deputy minister of Taiwan's National Development Council, January 2016

and environmental protection. Besides raising national income and upgrading the quality of life, the development plan aimed to raise Taiwan's status to that of a developed economy—a goal that was realized in 2002 when the country was admitted into the World Trade Organization (WTO).

In recent years, however, Taiwan's economy has stalled due to a number of factors. In 2015, economic growth was a mere 1 percent. Like so much else in Taiwan, the economy is affected by the island's complicated relationship with China. In addition, with its low birth rate of just over one child per woman—among the lowest in the world—Taiwan's population is aging quickly. The number of people over sixty-five are expected to account for nearly 20 percent of its total population by 2025. This will mean a smaller work force, declining tax revenues, and a growing segment of retired workers dependent on the government.

THE CHINA CONNECTION

Trade is Taiwan's lifeblood. Due to the political dispute between mainland China and Taiwan, direct trade between the two was banned until 1987. Taiwanese businesses got around this by indirectly trading with the mainland through Hong Kong.

Today, China is Taiwan's number one trade partner, accounting for more than 27 percent of all its exports. In 2006, China overtook the United States to become Taiwan's second-largest source of imports, now close on the heels of Japan. China is also the island's number one destination for foreign direct investment.

During his administration (2008—2016), President Ma Ying-jeou, of the KMT, pursued closer economic ties with China, which brought greater opportunities for Taiwan's economy. To be sure, Taiwan benefitted from China's rising economy, as Taiwanese high tech industries fulfilled large contracts with China. However, the island's increasing economic dependence on China worries many people, who see it as an entanglement that may prove impossible to unknot, leading inevitably to reunification with the Mainland under conditions that will be dictated by the People's Republic. At the same time, China's development of its own high tech industries has begun to replace its need for Taiwanese goods and services.

In 2016, Taiwan elected Tsai Ing-wen of the Democratic Progressive Party—which also won a majority in the Legislative Yuan—to be the next president. Her victory was seen as partly due to the Taiwanese people's dissatisfaction with the slowing economy. The public has demonstrated its frustration with stagnant wages, skyrocketing housing prices, and the difficulty of finding decent entry-level jobs. Because of these problems, Taiwan has suffered a "brain drain" as workers look overseas, and even to the mainland, for employment. In 2013, some six hundred thousand of Taiwan's twenty-three million people spent more than half of the year abroad. Three-quarters of those were in China. Other estimates put the figures even higher, saying one million or more people from Taiwan work overseas.

Tsai favors trade diversification to moderate Taiwan's growing dependency on China. For its part, the mainland government issued tough warnings to Taiwan immediately after the election. How Taiwan's new administration will influence Cross-Strait relations and how that will affect the economy remains to be seen.

A container ship heads out of the port of Kaohsiung.

INDUSTRY

The driving force behind Taiwan's economic miracle has been its dynamic industrial sector. In 2015, industry accounted for almost 35 percent of the gross domestic product (GDP)—that is, the total value of goods produced and services provided in a country in one year. The service industry, meanwhile, was almost two-thirds of GDP, at 63 percent.

TOURISM

Tourism is a major part of Taiwan's economy. Since easing restrictions on visitors from Mainland China in 2008, Taiwan has seen a large influx of Chinese tourists. In fact, they now make up the largest segment by far of Taiwan's tourists, with almost four million Mainland visitors traveling to Taiwan in 2014.

That same year, the island welcomed almost ten million international visitors, an increase of almost two million over the previous year. After the Chinese, Japanese tourists are next largest group.

Taipei is naturally a leading destination in itself, and hosts a number of top attractions, including the National Palace Museum, Chiang-Kai-shek Memorial Hall, and Taipei 101, the distinctive skyscraper that was the world's tallest building from 2004–2010. The Shilin Night Market and the Mengjia Longshan Temple, both also in Taipei, are popular. Outside of the capital city, Sun Moon Lake is a much-visited scenic region. National Parks and other wilderness areas show off Taiwan's spectacular natural beauty.

National Theater and Concert Hall in Taipei.

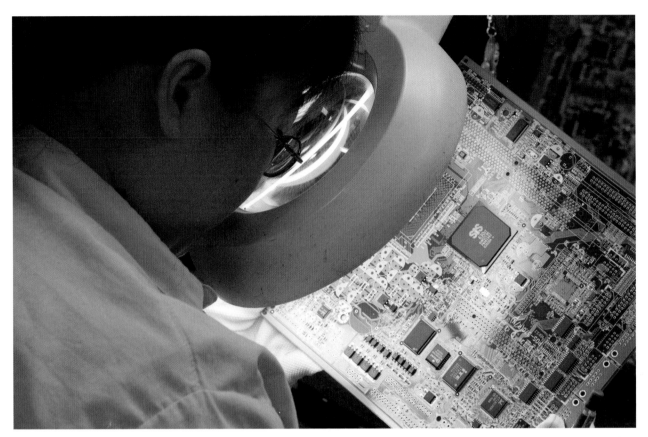

Among the heavy industrial goods manufactured are transportation equipment, electrical and electronic machinery, and metal and petrochemical products. Light industrial goods include beverages, tobacco, textiles, and clothing.

Earlier this century, the high-tech industry was one of Taiwan's shining stars. Its computer company Acer overtook Dell to become the world's second-largest personal computer maker. HTC, a Taiwanese device maker, had surged ahead of Apple to become the largest smartphone seller in the United States. Then, however, the tide turned—the PC market slumped and HCT went into a nosedive amid corruption charges against some its top executives. Since 2015, Taiwan's electronic exports have been falling. Analysts fault a lack of creativity—a focus on short-term fixes in lieu of long-term innovation—in the high tech industry with preventing it from building on the base it had already established.

A worker inspects a motherboard at a computer manufacturing company.

AGRICULTURE

Although it remains a significant sector of the Taiwanese economy, agriculture has decreased considerably in importance. Contributing to one-third of the economy in 1952, it only accounted for 1.9 percent of Taiwan's GDP in 2015. This trend is not unusual in an industrializing nation, and farm workers tend to earn low incomes. Still, a country has to feed its people. In 2013, Taiwan was able to meet only 32 percent of its food needs, and had to import the rest.

Only about one-quarter of Taiwan's land is suitable for farming. However, that land is cultivated very intensely. Most farms are small, however, and modernization has been slow. The agricultural sector has many problems and concerns as it tries to upgrade the industry—from free trade competition with lower-priced foreign goods to the use of chemical fertilizers and pesticides, new plant technologies, ecological conservation and sustainability, and labor shortages.

Pineapples grow on a farm in Taiwan.

In 2013, Taiwan's agriculture was a mixture of crops (48 percent), livestock (31 percent), fishing (21 percent) and forestry (0.1 percent). Rice is the principal food crop, and is grown along the western plain and in the south. Other food crops include sugar cane, sweet potatoes, bananas and other tropical fruits, vegetables, peanuts, soybeans, and wheat. Taiwan also grows tea and flowers.

Some farmers have gone organic to tap into that market, and agritourism is also a growing sector. In 2013, there were more than seventy-five recreation farming zones and 317 recreational farms had been licensed.

Visitors enjoy a day at Cingjing Farm in Nantou County.

MINERAL RESOURCES

Taiwan's coal reserves of about 110 million tons are located mainly in the northern counties, and its oil and natural gas reserves are located mostly in Hsinchu and Miaoli counties. As these mineral resources are insufficient to generate enough energy for total domestic demand, many rivers have been dammed to produce hydroelectric power. Marble, limestone, and asbestos are Taiwan's other mineral resources.

INTERNET LINKS

www.4hoteliers.com/news/story/15315
Tourism is an important contributor to China-Taiwan relations.

www.cia.gov/library/publications/the-world-factbook/geos/tw.html
The CIA World Factbook has up-to-date information about Taiwan's economy.

www.roughguides.com/destinations/asia/taiwan
This travel site offers a wide variety of photos of Taiwan's top tourist attractions.

ENVIRONMENT

A protester wears a mask during a 2015 demonstration in Taipei against the government's energy policies.

5

TAIWAN IS HOME TO APPROXIMATELY 150,000 different forms of life—1.5 percent of all life species found on Earth—out of which 30 percent are endemic to the country. This vast variety in flora and fauna is partly due to the country's location between three climatic zones, and to its varied topography.

To protect its diverse ecosystems, the Taiwan government has set aside part of the country's land area as part of a multi-tiered conservation system. This includes nine national parks—Taroko, Yushan (Jade Mountain), Kenting, Yangmingshan, Shei-Pa, Kinmen, Dongsha Atoll, an oceanic national park established in 2007, Taijiang, and South Penghu Marine National Park, the most recent, established in 2014—as well as several nature reserves, forest reserves, and wildlife refuges.

The government of Taiwan has actively promoted nature conservation since the 1980s. In 1981 it enacted the Cultural Heritage Preservation Act, which mandates the creation of nature reserves. In 1989 the Wildlife Conservation Act was enacted where 1,955 species of rare fauna were classified into three levels of protection—"endangered," "rare and valuable," and "requiring conservation measures."

FOREST RESERVES

About 72 percent of the four million acres (1.6 million hectares) of forestland in Taiwan are natural forests. Forest reserves are national forestlands recognized as possessing unique characteristics and preservation is emphasized over land development.

Under a forest conservation program launched in 1965, the Forestry Bureau surveys and identifies different kinds of representative ecosystems, rare plants, and animals. It also drafts plans for long-term study and educational tourism within protected nature areas. The Forestry Bureau operates a network of hostels in forest areas that are more than a day's journey from any city and these hostels are open to the public for a fee, depending on the services available and the length of stay.

ENDANGERED SPECIES

The Cultural Heritage Conservation Law prohibits hunting, fishing, collecting, logging, or other forms of destruction of designated rare and valuable animals and plants. Since 1982, twenty-three species of animals and eleven species of plants have been identified by the Council of Agriculture as rare and valuable. Many of these plants and animals are endemic to Taiwan and include the Formosan black bear, the Mikado pheasant, the Taiwan pleione, and the Taiwan amentotaxus.

The Formosan black bear, in fact, is a symbol of the country, and is protected by laws. Yet its existence is gravely threatened by poaching, habitat encroachment, lax law enforcement, and public indifference. The concept of animal rights is still new in Taiwan.

Urbanization and industrialization have taken their toll on the island's wildlife. Habitat destruction due to land development, pollution, excessive hunting, and logging has led to a dramatic reduction in the population of wild animals. Wildlife conservation was neglected during Taiwan's years of industrial development in the 1960s and 1970s. In 2013, Taiwan university researchers determined, after an intensive, four-year-long search, that the

The Formosan black bear is the largest land animal in Taiwan.

Formosan clouded leopard had become extinct on the island. In fact, the animal probably hasn't existed on Taiwan in at least one hundred years, but nevertheless, people held out hope that a small number might still be somewhere deep in the wilderness. The news that the leopard was truly gone caught the public's attention in a way that conservation efforts rarely do. The animal's demise was traced to the usual suspects: urbanization, poaching, and habitat destruction. Activists hope the clouded leopard case will spur the Taiwanese people to help save other species on the island—such as the Formosan black bear.

GOING GREEN

The Environmental Protection Agency (EPA) is the only government agency at the national level that is solely devoted to the environmental conservation movement in Taiwan. The responsibilities of the EPA include setting standards to regulate the amount of pollution and the drafting of environmental conservation laws. As an example to the rest of the country, the EPA issued a mandate in 2002 requiring all central government agencies (including state-owned enterprises and schools) and municipal agencies to initiate "green procurement" efforts—that is, 50 percent of the supplies procured by these agencies have to be environmentally friendly. Those who met the standards received a certification called a Green Mark. In 2002, with the implementation of such "green" purchasing measures, applications for the use of the Green Mark imprint increased nearly fourfold.

The EPA's Green Mark Program also encourages manufacturers to produce products that are recyclable and have low environmental impact—and it encourages customers to buy those products. As of 2015, more than 14,500 products had been certified to display the Green Mark logo.

In 2013, the Green Mark Program was extended to the service sector. The EPA now awards gold, silver, or bronze ratings to environmentally-conscious travel agencies, restaurants, cleaning services, car rentals, and car wash companies.

The Taiwanese government has also taken this green living concept to transportation, sustainable energy sources, and building standards.

FIGHTING POLLUTION

Being a small, densely-occupied island, Taiwan naturally has significant problems with pollution.

A protester displays a sign during a demonstration demanding the Taiwan government reduce air pollution in Taipei.

AIR POLLUTION Taiwan has some of the worst air pollution in Asia. In fact, the World Health Organization (WHO) ranked Taiwan last of the four East Asian countries known as the Asian Tigers, the other three being Singapore, Hong Kong, and South Korea. Air pollution levels are measured internationally according to the PM2.5 control standard, which Taiwan adopted in 2012. This standard measures the air density of fine particulate matter of 2.5 micrometers or less in diameter. This indicator is useful for predicting health risks from air pollution, as the particulate matter is inhaled and accumulates in the respiratory system.

In Taiwan, the main contributors to the problem are vehicular emissions, thermal power generators, steel plants and large-scale factories. Occasionally, pollution from mainland China, which also has a serious problem, drifts across the strait, blown by seasonal winds.

Taiwan's Air Pollution Control Act (enacted in 1975, revised in 2002) empowers the government to establish air-quality standards for different areas across Taiwan. The combat against air pollution heightened with the issuance of air-quality improvement measures, which include the articulation of tough emission standards for industrial plants and motor vehicles, regular exhaust inspections for motorcycles, the promotion of low-pollution transportation vehicles, as well as imposing strict standards on the composition of petroleum products, among other measures.

The result is that air quality in Taiwan is actually better than it used to be. Still, some people complain that the EPA does little more than issue warnings and advise people to stay indoors on bad air quality days. The EPA for its part, points to a series of Clean Air Action Plans for the period 2015 to 2020. The action plans are fortified with eight additional measures: promoting electric bikes (E-bikes), buses (E-buses), and trucks; fitting diesel cars with soot filters; installing natural gas boilers in hotels; installing riverbed fugitive dust prevention mechanisms; promoting cooperation with mainland China in improving air quality; and conducting research on fine particulate matter (PM2.5) control.

WATER POLLUTION Taiwan has 118 rivers and streams under government supervision, twenty-four of which provide the country with 85 percent of the water used by its citizens. Measures to ensure water quality include setting up water quality sampling stations throughout the country as well as placing thirteen of these rivers on a priority watch list.

The main pollutants of Taiwan's rivers are domestic sewage and industrial discharges. Urban communities are the main polluters, primarily because of the lack of comprehensive sewage systems. In 1991, the extent rate of public underground sewerage systems in Taiwan was merely 3 percent. After years of construction, the amount reached almost 11 percent in 2003. In the same year, the government incorporated the construction of public underground sewerage systems into its national "Water and Green Construction Plan." The hook-up rate to public underground sewerage systems reached 22.58 percent by 2009, with 47.8 percent of wastewater being properly treated. Much of the untreated water is still being discharged into rivers.

WASTE DISPOSAL AND RECYCLING

Before 1984, most people in Taiwan dumped their garbage randomly at different places, and the waste disposal facilities were simple and primitive. To manage the disposal of waste, the government built landfills and instituted a plan for recycling.

By 2008, the government claimed that almost 100 percent of waste was correctly disposed of. Incineration replaced landfills as the primary means of waste disposal. The government's goal now is to aim for a policy of Zero Waste, with the emphasis on waste minimization, recycling, and reuse, and says it expects to slash the volume of waste generated in Taiwan by 75 percent by 2020.

In Taipei recycling trucks visit the city's neighborhoods three times a week to collect recyclable materials. Large home appliances and furniture that may be reused are collected by appointment. Nonrecyclable garbage must be disposed of in special blue bags. The purchase price of the bags includes a special fee for disposing of the garbage. These efforts have succeeded in reducing Taipei's daily trash production by a third as well as increasing its recyclable trash collection threefold.

ENERGY SUSTAINABILITY

The government says it would like to adopt a sustainable approach to energy by developing renewable energy resources—primarily solar, wind and biomass energy and secondarily hydro and tidal energy. This is a huge challenge. In 2014, fossil fuels—oil, coal and natural gas—constituted 89.9 percent of all Taiwan's energy sources, while nuclear power contributed 8.3 percent, and power from renewable energy accounted for only 1.8 percent.

In 2009, the Legislative Yuan passed a renewable energy act aimed at promoting the use of renewable energy, boosting energy diversification, and helping reduce greenhouse gases. It aims for renewable energy to account for 15 percent of the nation's energy by 2025. President-elect Tsai Ing-wen said in January 2015 that her party aimed to phase out nuclear power in Taiwan by 2025 and to increase the share of renewable energy generation to 20 percent by that year.

CLIMATE CHANGE

The Republic of China lost its seat at the United Nations in 1971 when it was replaced by the People's Republic of China. Having both entities be members was and continues to be unacceptable to the PRC. Because of this, Taiwan has been unable to participate in the UN Framework Convention on Climate Change (UNFCCC), the international environmental treaty formed in 1994 to address issues dealing with greenhouse gas (GHG) emissions and climate change. Despite this exclusion, Taiwan continues to make its own efforts at combating the problem. In 2010, it approved a master plan, which in 2014 was renamed the Green Energy and Low Carbon Master Plan. The plan calls for "nationally appropriate mitigation actions" that are measurable, reportable, and verifiable in line with the UNFCCC Copenhagen Accord. It aims to reduce GHG emissions to 2005 levels by 2020 and to 2000 levels by 2025. Between 2010 and 2014, the Master Plan helped reduce CO_2 emissions by 28.2 million metric tons (31 million tons). Although CO_2 emissions fluctuate from year to year, they are steadily declining overall.

In June 2015, the Legislative Yuan passed the Greenhouse Gas Emission Reduction and Management Act, providing the government with a legal basis for taking action against climate change. The law sets a target of reducing Taiwan's GHG emissions volume to less than half its 2005 level by the year 2050. It also stipulates the establishment of a national action plan for climate change.

INTERNET LINKS

aqicn.org/map/taiwan
This interactive map shows the levels of air quality in Taiwan in real time.

www.bbc.com/news/world-asia-pacific-12208493
"Taiwan endangered species focus of new awareness" examines Taiwan's animal abuse and protection.

www.ey.gov.tw/en/cp.aspx?n=0775D186E2307F53
The Republic of China Yearbook 2015 page on Environmental Protection has a good deal of information on the government's goals and accomplishments.

www.taipeitimes.com/News/feat/archives/2015/12/20/2003635208
This article looks at how Taiwan's inability to be a member of the UN hampers its climate change activists.

TAIWANESE

A native girl performs a traditional aboriginal dance for Christmas.

6

THE 23.4 MILLION PEOPLE OF TAIWAN are essentially urban dwellers. In recent years the boundaries of urban areas have extended beyond the official limits of major cities, leading to the formation of large metropolitan areas that are now home to more than three-quarters, or 77 percent, of Taiwan's total population. Since industrial development took off in the 1960s, the number of rural residents has dwindled as more families leave their farms to work in industry.

THE CHINESE IN TAIWAN

The majority of people in Taiwan (about 98 percent) are Han Chinese, the dominant ethnic group of China. Han is the name commonly given to the Chinese people who originated from the central plains of China. Among the Han Chinese in Taiwan, there are substantial differences between native Taiwanese and mainlanders.

NATIVE TAIWANESE The native Taiwanese are those whose families arrived in Taiwan from the Chinese mainland before 1945. Few Chinese immigrants came to Taiwan during the Japanese colonial period.

Sankeng Old Street in Taoyuan City is a traditional Hakka community.

Therefore, there is, in effect, a fifty-year gap between those who arrived before and after 1945, which makes it easy to understand the differences and distinctions between mainlanders and the native Taiwanese who make up 84 percent of the population and are mostly either Hakkas (HAH-kahs), or from the Fujian and Guangdong provinces.

The Hakkas originally came from Hunan province in China. For centuries they were a wandering people, and the name Hakka means "guest," suggesting temporary occupation. Within China many moved to Guangdong and Fujian provinces to escape the northern tribes that had invaded their home provinces; eventually many of them migrated to Taiwan. Hakkas were among the first migrants to arrive from mainland China in the twelfth century. Most of the Hakkas now live in northeastern Taiwan.

MAINLANDERS   The mainlanders are so called because they are the immigrants who fled the mainland just before or soon after the Communist victory there in 1949. The term also applies to their descendants. When the 1.5 million mainlanders first arrived in Taiwan, their impact on society was great. Almost overnight the population of Taiwan swelled from 6 million to 7.5 million. The immigrants occupied many of the government and administrative positions in Taiwan and, in effect, controlled the government.

ETHNIC UNREST   Relations between the native Taiwanese and the mainlanders have not always been easy. The February 28 incident in 1947 was the worst and most violent expression of antagonism between the two groups. The native Taiwanese resented the fact that mainlanders, while accounting for less than 15 percent of the population, had taken over the government and the island itself. This situation only began changing in the 1970s, when President Chiang Ching-kuo allowed more native Taiwanese to enter the political arena, and chose Lee Teng-hui, a native Taiwanese, to be vice president. When Lee became president in 1988 after Chiang's death, this was regarded as a momentous event in Taiwan's political history.

There remains some lingering resentment between the native Taiwanese and the mainlanders, who are sometimes thought to be arrogant. However, as many of the original mainlanders who came to Taiwan in 1949 are replaced by a new generation, greater assimilation between the two groups is occurring. Young Taiwanese pay little attention to ethnic differences, while increasing instances of intermarriage between mainlanders and the native Taiwanese have also helped to narrow the remaining gap between them.

THE ABORIGINES

Taiwan has approximately half a million aborigines, or *yuan zhu min* (YOO-an Ju min), meaning original people—the indigenous people of the island. They are of Austronesian stock, having arrived in Taiwan thousands of years ago from regions as far away as Easter Island, Madagascar, and New Zealand. They currently make up about 2 percent of the entire Taiwanese population.

Aboriginal women are dressed in traditional costumes in Kaohsiung.

The indigenous tribes represented in that 2 percent are the Amis, Atayal, Bunun, Kavalan, Paiwan, Puyuma, Rukai, Saisiat, Sakizaya, Seediq, Thao, Truku, Tsou, and Yami tribes. In 2014, the Taiwanese government recognized two additional aboriginal tribes, the Hla'alua and the Kanakanavu, bringing the total number to sixteen. The Ami group is the largest of them, accounting for more than one-third of the indigenous population.

The aborigines are physically different from the Han Chinese in that they tend to have darker skin, bigger eyes, and sharper noses. Originally they lived in the plains, but with the arrival of the mainland Chinese over the centuries, they gradually retreated into the mountains. Their traditional occupations were farming, hunting, animal husbandry, and fishing. They are still involved in crafts such as weaving and metalwork.

At Sun Moon Lake in the Central Range, the Formosan Aboriginal Culture Village houses a model recreation of aboriginal villages representing the various tribes. Besides carrying on with their traditional lifestyle based on agriculture and hunting, some tribes have turned to making traditional crafts to attract tourist dollars. However, some aborigines are fed up with being treated like tourist attractions and object to having their lives put on display.

AMIS The largest aboriginal tribe in Taiwan is the Amis. They are found mainly in the eastern region of Taiwan from Hualien to Taitung. The Amis have a matriarchal society in which the oldest woman in the family is the head of the household. The family name is carried on through the women, so children inherit their mother's name. When men get married, they traditionally move in with their wives' families.

Traditional Ami homes are thatched huts with wooden beams. Most houses are large communal dwellings because extended families live together. The Amis have a reverence for nature and worship gods of nature. They have many rites and ceremonies, the most important being the harvest festival held in July and August each year.

Farmers from the Amis tribe hold up day lily buds in Cihara'ay, Hualien County.

WARRIORS OF THE RAINBOW

The 2011 movie, Warriors of the Rainbow: Seediq Bale, *is unusual for several reasons. The film by Taiwanese director Wei Te-Sheng is a historical drama about Taiwan's aborigines. It stars a number of aboriginal actors, many with no previous acting experience, and was the most expensive production in Taiwanese cinema history. Originally a two-part film running four-and-a-half hours, the movie was trimmed to a single, two-and-a-half-hour cut for international release.*

The story is based on a true, little-known event in 1930 called the Wushe Incident that occurred when Taiwan was under Japanese control. After years of being mistreated by the Japanese, a coalition of aboriginal Seediq mountain tribes mounted a surprise rebellion in an attempt to drive the Japanese out of aboriginal homelands. The Japanese responded in a particularly brutal way, using mustard gas bombs to flush the rebels out of the forests. Of the 1,200 Seediq directly involved in the uprising, 644 died, and 290 committed suicide to avoid being taken alive. However, a few months later, the tribe's village was attacked and all the remaining men over fifteen were beheaded.

Wushe Incident Memorial Statue,

ATAYAL The Atayal people are distributed mainly over the northern parts of Taiwan. Some members live in the Taroko National Park. Like other aboriginals, the Atayal live by farming and hunting. Unlike the matriarchal Ami, Atayal men take their wives and children to live with their families. The Atayal religion is based on a belief in *utux* (OOH-tooks), or supernatural spirits and the spirits of the dead.

A member of the Saisiyat tribe performs at the Ai Jin Li festival in Wu Fong.

YAMI AND SAISIYAT They are among the smallest tribal groups in Taiwan. The Yami peoples' homeland is Lanyu, or Orchid Island, but many have left to live in Taiwan because of a lack of job opportunities on Lanyu. They are mainly fishing people who supplement their catch by breeding pigs and growing taro, sweet potato, yam, and millet. Traditionally, men and women have different roles—the men prepare the fields for cultivation, build boats, go fishing, build homes, weave baskets, and make pottery; the women tend to the crops and harvest them, take care of domestic affairs, and weave cloth. Being a fishing community, the Yami are famous for their beautifully carved and painted canoes.

The Yami also have a matriarchal system. Women can have trial marriages for one month; if a husband does not prove his worth by contributing to his wife's family, his wife can divorce him and look for a new husband.

The Saisiyat are mainly agriculturalists and foresters whose culture has been strongly influenced by their neighbors, the Atayal aborigines. Three or four households of the same name usually make up one Saisiyat settlement. A few neighboring settlements may join to form a village with shared farming land and amenities.

TRADITIONAL DRESS

For most Taiwanese today, including aborigines, traditional costumes are mostly just for festivals and other special occasions. Western-style clothing is the choice for everyday wear.

On some occasions, Chinese women may wear the traditional *cheongsam* (also called a *chipao*), a long, slim-fitting, knee- or ankle-length dress with a slit at each side and a high mandarin collar. The dress is usually made of a rich Chinese silk and has a beautiful floral print. It is often sleeveless or has short sleeves, although long sleeves are also possible. The *changshan* is the traditional dress for men. It consists of three pieces—a black, waist-length jacket with a Mandarin collar and long, loose sleeves; a dark blue underskirt that extends to the knees and has slits at the sides; and long, black, loose-fitting trousers. Both the male and female versions are modified forms of traditional Ching Dynasty dress.

More women than men wear traditional clothes. At weddings, for instance, the bride usually changes from a Western-style dress into a cheongsam at the wedding reception, but the groom continues to wear his Western-style suit. Among the wedding guests, it is usually the older people who wear traditional clothes.

A young woman wears a cheongsam and holds a paper parasol.

INTERNET LINKS

lifeoftaiwan.com/about-taiwan/people
This site offers an overview of Taiwan's diverse people.

thetaiwanphotographer.com/projects/taiwanese-aboriginal-tribes
This photo gallery portrays modern aboriginal people dressed in traditional tribal wedding attire.

travel.cnn.com/hong-kong/visit/seediq-bale-401232
This is an interview with the director and indigenous actors of *Seediq Bale*.

LIFESTYLE

A family rides on a motorcycle in Taipei.

THE TAIWANESE PEOPLE ENJOY A comfortable lifestyle, influenced by Western culture but guided by deeply traditional Chinese values. They, especially young people, tend to love all things Western—the food, the clothes, the music, the shopping, and so forth. Indeed, Taiwan's prosperous material culture, with its commercial aspects, can seem quite Western, at least superficially. Taiwan also mirrors the West in its democracy, free press, and free elections. Technologically, Taiwan is very modern and industrialized. However, it would be a mistake to assume that Taiwan is just like the United States or Canada or a European country. Its culture is inherently Chinese, and this is reflected in everyday life.

7

The color white symbolizes death and is used at funerals instead of the black common in the West. At weddings, red is a popular color because it represents good luck.

CONFUCIANISM

Confucian ethics are the single most important element in Taiwanese people's values and beliefs. Confucianism is based on the teachings of China's greatest teacher and philosopher, Confucius (551—479 BCE). Although many of the practices associated with Confucianism have been mistakenly called a religion, in reality it is a code of conduct. Confucianism focuses on maintaining harmony in the world. Everyone has a particular place in their society and in the world, and if people respect preset rules of social behavior, the result will be social harmony.

Confucius prescribed a code of behavior for five specific categories of relationships—loyalty of a subject to a ruler, of a son to his father, of a younger brother to an elder brother, of a wife to a husband, and of one friend to another. This code was a set of rules that taught people about the sort of behavior required in each relationship. The respect and loyalty that are integral parts of each relationship are fundamental Confucian values aimed at strengthening social harmony. Confucianism is therefore often called "a code of conduct, a guide to morality and good government." All aspects of Taiwanese and Chinese life are, to some extent, influenced by the teachings of Confucius.

Filial piety, called *xiào* (see-ow), or respect and obedience to one's family elders, is one of the most important Confucian virtues. It operates as a strong force binding families together in Taiwan. Increasing Westernization has not eroded this force.

THE IMPORTANCE OF FAMILY

The Confucian focus on group solidarity and harmony is best seen in the family model. The family is not only the most important unit of society in Taiwan, but it is also the strongest and most cohesive social unit. Children are brought up to respect the family structure and to understand that their primary duty is to the family. This ensures that filial piety is perpetuated and that families remain close-knit. Families also feature strongly in Taiwanese and Chinese society as a source of comfort and support in times of illness or trouble for individual members.

In the traditional family structure, extended families often live together, so that a single household may have as many as ten to fifty members. It used to be very common for at least three generations to live together, with the grandparents, adult children, and grandchildren all residing under the same roof. At one time, having many children was considered to be a way of honoring the family ancestors. Before family planning became commonly practiced, couples sometimes had as many as eight to ten children; as each of those children grew up and had their own large families, a single extended family could have up to one hundred members.

Large extended families are no longer the norm in urban Taiwan, where living constraints have led to the increasing prevalence of nuclear families. In crowded and expensive cities, especially in Taipei, the cost of maintaining large households is just too much for the average family to bear. It is now common for sons and daughters to get their own apartments when they marry and start their own families. As such, aging parents sometimes live alone, although they often move in with their children once there are grandchildren.

A mother and her young son play at the seashore.

CONFUCIUS: THE TEACHER OF ALL GENERATIONS

China's most famous teacher and philosopher, Kong fūzi (called Confucius), was born in mainland China in 551 BCE during what is known as the Warring States period. This was a time of great anarchy and confusion in China as different warlords struggled for power.

Confucius's father died when he was very young, so he was brought up by his mother and was largely self-educated. He was very disturbed by the political and social chaos of those times and believed they were caused by corrupt officials who had abandoned the correct codes of conduct. Although Confucius tried to get a job in the civil service that would allow him to implement his ideas, he was not very successful. So he decided instead to travel around the country to spread his beliefs on the value of humanitarian behavior, loyalty to the family, and respect for authority.

Three of his most important teachings focused on the concepts of li *(lee), meaning ritual or etiquette;* yi, *or righteousness; and* ren *(jehn), meaning kindness and benevolence to all human beings. He believed that if everyone practiced ren, the world would be a better place. According to Confucius, the ideal man should be a* junzi *(JUHN-zee), a perfect man who lives according to his principles.*

In those days education was available only to rich noblemen. Confucius defied tradition by opening a school that accepted all pupils regardless of wealth or status. Over a period of forty years, he taught some three thousand pupils from all backgrounds on the subjects of ritual, music, archery, driving chariots, history, and mathematics. Many of his teachings survive today in a collection called The Analects of Confucius.

Confucius died in 479 BCE, but his influence has not diminished. He is remembered and venerated in China and Taiwan as the Great Sage who established a code of conduct that forms the core of Chinese culture and lifestyle. His teachings have survived the test of time for 2,500 years. Every child in present-day Taiwan learns about Confucius's teachings. Every year on September 28 the entire island of Taiwan celebrates the birthday of this great teacher.

Family size is also shrinking, and most married couples nowadays tend to have only one or two children.

Until recently, Taiwan was a predominantly agricultural society. Women, as well as men, were workers, particularly in family farming. However, men were more likely to engage in trade and other forms of nonagricultural, waged labor. As more women now work outside of family farming and are financially independent, their role in the family is rapidly changing. More women are resisting the traditional thinking that their place is confined to the home. The role of the head of the household has also been redefined in modern Taiwanese society. Fathers once had absolute authority in the family and made all the decisions, but today their sons and daughters also expect to have a say in family matters, mainly because they may be better educated than the father.

The role of grandparents has also changed. Previously, they were considered the guardians of wisdom in extended families, and their opinions were sought after and respected. As many of the elder generation now live apart from their children and grandchildren, they have less influence in guiding family members. The traditional Chinese concept of family harmony has, to some extent, been eroded by an urban lifestyle. Nonetheless, grandparents continue to play a big role in rearing children. Daycare, nannies, and babysitters are rare in Taiwan because in most families grandparents are happy to take care of the youngsters when the parents are busy.

CHILDREN AND THE AGED

A major part of Taiwanese family life revolves around the children, and parents sometimes pamper them by giving in to their demands. Many traditional ideas about children remain. Sons are usually more cherished than daughters as they carry on the family name and perform the filial role of caring for elderly parents.

The extent to which children are cherished in Taiwan can be seen in the Children's Welfare Law, instituted to protect children. Unborn children are protected in a clause that prohibits pregnant mothers from smoking, drinking, or consuming any drug or substance that could put an unborn child in danger. Parents are not allowed to leave children under the age of six unsupervised, and parents who deprive children of the compulsory nine years of education can face legal prosecution.

Heavily influenced by Confucian tradition, Taiwanese people tend to respect the elderly, who are believed to have acquired wisdom after a lifetime of experience. Filial piety also reinforces this respect, and most Taiwanese feel an obligation to look after their elderly parents and relatives.

SOCIAL INTERACTIONS

A unique cultural characteristic of the Taiwanese is *ren qing wei* (RHEN ching WAY). Loosely translated, this means "the flavor of human feeling." It is a concept difficult to define in words but is seen in the appreciation of social relationships and experiences. It's a sense of one's innate ability to connect with another person, in social situations or business transactions. Social interactions that are imbued with sincerity, warmth, and civility are said to be expressions of *ren qing wei*. Friendliness and generosity to strangers, duty, and correct behavior are all part of this "flavor of human feeling."

Guanxi (GWAHN see) is another term that has no English translation. It roughly means interpersonal connections or network, and refers to the relationships between people in an extended family, in business, and in social situations that are often relied on to get things done. The person performing a favor can call on his or her guanxi at any time for a favor in return. The guanxi web of obligations can be complex and far-reaching.

"Keeping face" or "saving face" is another important characteristic of Chinese society. Basically, it is the idea of upholding a person's prestige and dignity in society, and it is important to everyone, both rich and poor.

WEDDINGS

Although the Taiwanese lifestyle has, to some extent, been influenced by Western trends, weddings and funerals are occasions when Chinese customs, traditions, and values still prevail. Until two generations ago, many marriages in Taiwan were arranged by the couple's parents. Sometimes the bride and groom might not even have seen each other until the wedding. But with a more open and modern society, most people now choose their spouses. Nonetheless, parents still play some role in bringing young people together in a formal meeting when a young man and woman are introduced with the family members present. If they like each other, they begin to date.

When a couple decides to get engaged, their parents consult astrologers to determine whether the match is a good one and to choose an auspicious wedding date. To formalize the engagement, the fiancée is formally introduced to her prospective husband's family and serves them sweet tea. In return, she is given gifts of money in small red envelopes called *hongbao* (HOHNG bow). At the end of this ceremony, rings are exchanged, and there is a formal banquet attended by the whole family.

The wedding ceremony takes place at the favorable date and time chosen by the astrologer. The groom goes to the bride's house, where the couple has a farewell meal, symbolizing the last meal the bride takes in her familial home. Upon reaching the groom's house, the couple must first pay respects to the family ancestors by burning incense at the family altar. After the wedding ceremony, a banquet rounds off the celebrations. Family and friends bring gifts of money in hongbao. During the banquet they toast the couple and wish them happiness.

A newlywed couple accepts gifts of hongbao.

FUNERALS

Chinese death customs involve elaborate rituals prior to and during cremations or burials, but the rituals do not end there. The Taiwanese believe that a person becomes a spirit after death. Therefore, certain rites must be performed to cater to the needs of the deceased's spirit. Before the funeral, the family bows and kneels before the open coffin. They wear white clothes made of rough cloth or burlap to show their grief. A seven-week mourning period is customary, at the end of which offerings are made to the deceased—sacrificial paper money, paper cars, paper clothes, paper houses, and other material goods are ritually burned in the belief that they will offer the departed an adequate lifestyle in the spirit world.

THE STATUS OF WOMEN

In traditional Chinese society, women were considered to be of a lower social status than men. Confucius taught that a woman's primary role was to serve her husband and family. The ideal qualities for women were passivity and submissiveness.

However, women in modern Taiwanese society have made tremendous strides through higher education and better opportunities, and more Taiwanese women are working in the business, government, and education sectors than ever before. In 2015, 45 percent of Taiwanese women held higher education degrees compared to only 39.3 percent of men. Although they have seen their pay rates rise, women's hourly rate of pay is only 85 percent of men's, on average, which means Taiwanese career women need to work an additional fifty-five days a year to get pay equal to men's.

Although the constitution provides for equality of the sexes, in reality many traditional attitudes regarding women's place in society still persist, and women in Taiwan are a long way from being on an equal footing with men.

THE IMPORTANCE OF EDUCATION

Following the Confucian emphasis on learning and the traditional respect that the Chinese have for scholars, education has always been greatly valued in Taiwan. According to the Educational Budget Allocation and Management Act, updated in 2011, the education budget must equal at least 22.5 percent of the national budget. The government makes a concerted effort to ensure equal educational opportunities for all—children from low-income families receive free textbooks and financial aid.

Until recently, compulsory education in Taiwan lasted only nine years, until the end of junior high school. However, in 2014 Taiwan extended compulsory education to last a full twelve years, through the end of senior high school. Elementary education is compulsory for all children from age six to twelve, and almost 100 percent of children in this age group attend school. Elementary schoolchildren learn subjects such as language, science, arithmetic, civics, arts, music, and physical education.

Junior high school lasts three years. Besides continuing with the learning of subjects taught in elementary schools, students also study a foreign language, for example English, and other subjects, such as mathematics, biology, chemistry, physics, and history. In senior high school, which lasts three years, students have three main options upon graduation: move on to a university or college; attend a two-year junior college; or enroll in a four-year institute of technology after one year of work—provided that the candidates have passed the relevant qualifying examinations.

To gain admission at universities and colleges, students from senior high schools and vocational schools have to sit for a joint university entrance examination. Competition is very stiff. Among the courses offered in higher education are liberal arts, law, business, physical sciences, engineering and industrial management, life sciences, biological engineering, agriculture, medicine, and applied agricultural sciences.

In the twenty-first century, the focus of Taiwan's educational system has been on the development of higher education. In 2014, there were more than 163 universities and colleges in Taiwan, and nearly 70 percent of Taiwan's young people ages eighteen to twenty-two pursued higher education, the second highest rate in world after South Korea. Post graduate education has also surged, with one out of 3.7 undergraduates attending graduate school. This has led to nearly sixty thousand students graduating from master's programs and four thousand from doctoral programs annually in recent years.

As of 2014 Taiwan had a high literacy rate of 98.5 percent. Most illiterate people belong to the older generation. Some did not attend school because of disabilities. Special educational policies now cater to this segment of the population—special schools serve the needs of the physically and mentally challenged, and supplementary schools provide education for adults who missed out on schooling in their earlier years.

Chinese Medicine is an approach to healing rooted in 2,500 years of Eastern Taoist tradition. It takes a very different view of disease and wellness than Western medical practice. Today, the two approaches are available in Taiwan under the public healthcare insurance program.

Traditional Chinese Medicine (TCM) is based on the concept of the qi (chee)—the body's vital energy. Health is a state of harmony and balance in the qi; disease results when the qi falls out of balance, or disharmony. The health of the qi is found in the balance between the forces of yin, the negative energy, and yang, the positive energy. When the two forces are out of balance, the qi is blocked and cannot flow freely. The person becomes ill.

The TCM practitioner applies any of a number of therapies to unblock the patient's qi and achieve inner harmony. These therapies may include herbal medicines, acupuncture, and reflexology.

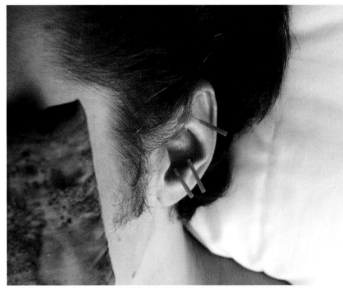

In acupuncture, the therapist inserts thin needles into the skin at certain points on the body, and manipulates those needles to stimulate the flow of qi. It is a pain relief therapy, among other things, that has proven popular in the United States and other Western countries, where it is sometimes used to treat chronic lower back pain and other symptoms that Western medicine often fails to help.

Reflexology involves massaging pressure points in the feet and hands to relieve ailments in other parts of the body. It is believed that the feet and hands contain pressure points linked to the body's internal organs through the circulatory, nervous, and energy systems. Stimulating these pressure points through massage stimulates the internal organs themselves.

HEALTH CARE AND SOCIAL SERVICES

Since the 1960s, Taiwan's government has invested large sums in improving and expanding the island's health services. As a result, the Taiwanese have access to a comprehensive health-care system. The improvements in health have led to rising life expectancy among the population—from fifty-three years for men and fifty-six years for women in 1951 to seventy-seven years for men and eighty-three years for women in 2015.

In the 1950s Taiwan's major health problems and causes of death among the population were gastroenteritis, pneumonia, and communicable diseases. But with improved health care, cancer and heart disease now register as the major causes of death, very much similar to the health patterns in advanced countries like the United States. In fact, some of Taiwan's main public health concerns today are pollution and industrial hazards. The growing aging population is also a cause for concern, as this puts a strain on the national health system.

In 1995, Taiwan launched the National Health Insurance program (NHI), providing universal health care to all its citizens, in both Chinese and Western-style medicine. It has since been called one of the best universal healthcare systems in the world.

INTERNET LINKS

english.moe.gov.tw/public/Attachment/59411143671.pdf
The Ministry of Education offers a PDF in English, "Education in Taiwan, 2015—2016."

www.nhi.gov.tw/Resource/
webdata/21717_1_20120808UniversalHealthCoverage.pdf
This is an overview of Taiwan's universal health care coverage.

www.patheos.com/Library/Confucianism
This site offers information on Confucianism under a variety of subtopics.

RELIGION

People visit a temple topped with a huge golden Buddha in Kaoshiung, Taiwan.

8

MOST PEOPLE IN TAIWAN IDENTIFY with a combination of compatible beliefs—a mix of Mahayana Buddhism, Confucianism, Taoism, and local traditions. Of the major world religions, Buddhism has the strongest influence in Taiwan, but Buddhist beliefs and practices also merge to a large extent with folk beliefs and other Chinese religions, such as Taoism.

Because of this overlap, attempts at deriving statistics about the numbers of people who practice a certain religion in Taiwan are difficult, and the results are quite different from one survey to another. The *CIA World Factbook* simply states that 93 percent of Taiwanese observe "a mixture of Buddhist and Taoist" religions, with another 4.5 percent being Christian, and 2.5 percent "other."

Although many people in Taiwan may not belong to any religious group or have a formal place of worship, they still subscribe to traditional beliefs. Most homes have family altars and shrines where they perform the rites of ancestral worship: incense is burned, and offerings are made to the gods or spirits.

Burning incense
is a part of
the Buddhist
prayer ritual and
represents a
sacred offering.

BUDDHISM

Although Buddhism is considered a religion, it is in essence more a philosophy of life, or a way of life. Unlike many religions, it is non-theistic, meaning it has no god or gods. It also puts less emphasis on belief or faith, and more on practice.

Buddhism was founded in India in the sixth century BCE by Siddhartha Gautama, who was disillusioned by the misery and injustice he observed in the world, and who attained spiritual enlightenment after meditating for many years. The name *Buddha* means "The Enlightened One." Buddha taught that craving and desire were the source of human suffering and that meditation and the search for truth could lead to spiritual enlightenment. Buddhism worldwide is practiced in two forms—Mahayana Buddhism, which is found in China, Taiwan, Japan, Korea, and some other countries, aspires to universal enlightenment, not only out of a sense of compassion, but because the individual cannot be separated from the other. Theraveda Buddhism,

BUDDHISM WITH A SOCIAL CONSCIENCE

A new form of "humanistic" Buddhism has become popular in Taiwan. This approach focuses on the core Buddhist principals—speaking good words, thinking good thoughts, and doing good deeds—and applying them within the family and also to helping others.

The Buddhist Compassion Relief Tzu Chi Foundation, founded in 1966 by a thirty-year-old female monk, Dharma Master Cheng Yen, is the largest and best-known charitable organization in Taiwan. It has sent emergency relief to disasters in more than eighty-four countries. There are also several other socially engaged Buddhist groups in Taiwan, including Fo Guang Shan (Buddha's Light Mountain), Fagushan (Dharma Drum Mountain), and others.

Changing the way Buddhism is practiced has not only led to a revival of the religion in Taiwan, but to its expansion overseas.

more common in Southeast Asia, aspires to individual enlightenment through contemplation and self-purification.

Buddhism came to China from India in the first century CE, but only became established as a major religion during the Sui (581–618 CE) and Tang (618–907 CE) dynasties. In the late Ming (1368–1644) and early Qing (1644–1911) dynasties, immigrants from the mainland took the religion to Taiwan. After Koxinga drove the Dutch out of Taiwan in 1662, more Buddhist monks came to the island. In the seventeenth and eighteenth centuries a number of Buddhist temples were built, some of which still survive.

TAOISM

Taoism originated in China 2,500 years ago, at about the same time that Confucius taught his ideas. Its founder is Lao Tzu (meaning "Old One"), whose teachings are contained in a book, the *Tao Teh Ching* (Dow de jing). Taoism advocates living a life of simplicity and passivity by following *tao*, meaning the guiding path that leads to immortality. With the spread of Taoism, Lao Tzu achieved the status of an immortal being and was later regarded as a Taoist god. Other people who lived in harmony with nature were also

believed to have become immortal and were worshipped as gods.

As with Buddhism, Taoism was brought to Taiwan by immigrants from the mainland. To some extent, it has merged with Buddhist and folk beliefs in Taiwan. Unlike Buddhist temples, which maintain a simple austerity, Taoist temples in Taiwan are the sites of elaborate rites where Taoist priests offer thanksgiving prayers to the gods and pray for prosperity and happiness. Since Taoists believe in supernatural spirits,

Young women perform a folk dance honoring the Earth god.

Taoist priests are often called upon to exorcise evil spirits and bless homes and offices.

FOLK RELIGION

Folk religion, too, arrived in Taiwan with the early immigrants. In common with the Chinese characteristic of merging beliefs and philosophies, Taiwanese folk religion absorbed many beliefs from Buddhism and Taoism. It also has a number of gods and goddesses, including Kuan Yin, the goddess of mercy. Ma Zu, the goddess of the sea, is particularly popular in Taiwan, where there are more than seven hundred temples dedicated to her. Annual processions are held in her honor, the largest being the Dajia Ma Zu Pilgrimage, which winds through several cities and counties in central and southern Taiwan for eight or nine days in the third lunar month—usually in March or April.

The supreme deity in folk religion is the god of heaven. Other gods include the house god and the Earth god. Many gods were once mortal men and women who, after their deaths, were elevated to the status of gods because they had achieved some fame or honor during their lives. For instance, Kuankung was a faithful friend of the emperor in the third century CE. His integrity and loyalty earned him the status of a folk god. A crucial part of Chinese religious belief focuses on the philosophy that people are rewarded for good deeds by becoming gods and entering heaven after they die. Those guilty of evil deeds are punished by being transformed into ghosts and sent to hell. Both gods and ghosts must be appeased and worshipped by the living. Departed ancestors are also believed to have power. As angry ancestors can cause bad luck, their descendants make offerings to keep their spirits happy.

SPIRIT WORLD OF THE ABORIGINES

The aborigines of Taiwan believe in spirits that live in inanimate objects, such as stones and trees. These are said to be the spirits of people who have died. After death they were liberated from their human bodies to dwell in the spirit world. A great part of aboriginal religious ritual involves appeasing these spirits as they can unleash destruction on humanity when any wrongdoing is committed. On the other hand, when people live according to the rules of society, the spirits help them and grant them their wishes.

The Ami believe that, once upon a time, a male god was born from the splitting of mountains and a female god was born from a tree after a flood in a bamboo forest. These two gods are believed to be the ancestors of human beings. The Saisiyat believe that in ancient times there was a flood that drowned everyone. The only survivor was cut into pieces by the gods and thrown into the sea. From these pieces human beings were born again.

OTHER RELIGIONS

Yiguandao is the third most popular religion in Taiwan. Literally meaning "The Religion of One Unity," Yiguandao draws not only on traditional Chinese teachings but also from major religions, such as Buddhism, Taoism, Christianity, Islam, Judaism, and Hinduism. It preaches that, by uncovering a single set of universal truths inherent in these major religions, people can live in peace and harmony.

Christianity came to Taiwan in the sixteenth century with the arrival of the Europeans. The Dutch introduced Protestantism, and the Spanish priests spread Roman Catholicism. Some past ROC presidents were Christians, at

One of the most important deities in the Chinese pantheon is Kuan Yin, who was once a young woman called Miau Chan. According to legend, Miau Chan was a very kind and compassionate girl. When she grew up, her father wanted her to get married, but Miau Chan chose to enter a nunnery. When her father tried to discourage her from this by making sure she had to do all the most difficult chores, Miau Chan became even more determined to devote her life to religion. Finally her father had her killed.

Miau Chan's goodness of spirit was so strong that the gods sent her back to earth, where she saved her father from a fatal illness by sacrificing herself. When her father discovered this, he was overcome with remorse, gave up all his worldly goods, and became a Buddhist.

After this Miau Chan became known as Kuan Yin, or "One Who Sees and Hears the Cry of the Human World." She symbolizes the greatest loving kindness and compassion. Interestingly, Kuan Yin is a goddess for both Buddhists and Taoists. She is especially worshipped by women who want to have children and by people seeking forgiveness for wrongdoings.

Lungshan Temple in Lukang, Taiwan

In Taiwan, more than five hundred temples are dedicated to Kuan Yin. Among the most famous is the Lungshan temple in Taipei, dating back to the eighteenth century. Images of Kuan Yin usually show the goddess holding a vase containing the dew of compassion. According to legend, a sprinkling of this dew can heal illnesses miraculously.

least nominally. The Taiwan government estimates about 4.5 percent of Taiwan's population is Christian, about half Protestant and half Catholic. Nearly all of Taiwan's aborigines profess Christianity—about 70 percent Presbyterian, the rest Catholic—as missionaries have largely succeeded in wiping out the native religions.

The country's Muslim community numbers about sixty thousand. Some of these Muslims are descendants of soldiers who came to Taiwan as part of Koxinga's army, while others came from northern China in 1949, after the Communist takeover of the mainland.

INTERNET LINKS

www.aljazeera.com/indepth/features/2014/12/islam-taiwan-lost-tradition-2014123173558796270.html
This is an article about Islam in Taiwan.

www.bbc.com/news/world-asia-25772194
This article discusses a new humanistic form of Buddhism gaining popularity in Taiwan.

lifeoftaiwan.com/about-taiwan/religion
Life of Taiwan offers a short overview of religions on the island.

www.myseveralworlds.com/2013/08/04/fo-guang-shan-buddhist-monastery-in-kaohsiung-southern-taiwan
This Taiwan travel site has a nice section with good photos on the Fo Guang Shan Monastery.

www.pbs.org/edens/thailand/buddhism.htm
This introduction to Buddhism is a quick overview of its basic tenets.

www.tzuchi.us
This is the site of the Buddhist Compassion Relief Tzu Chi Foundation.

LANGUAGE

9

A LTHOUGH PEOPLE SOMETIMES refer to the "Chinese language," or say that someone "speaks Chinese," there is, in fact, no language named Chinese. However, with Mandarin being the official language of both China and Taiwan, it has come to be called Standard Chinese.

In Taiwan, the Mandarin language is called *kuo yu* (GWOH ewe-ee), meaning "national language." It's one of the major branches of the Sino-Tibetan family of languages and is characterized by the use of tones to distinguish between the meanings of words. It is a monosyllabic language—each syllable has a different meaning.

In written form, Mandarin uses traditional Chinese characters, a form of pictographs. Though many languages from ancient civilizations went through stages where they were written in pictorial form, the Chinese written language is unique in being the only major writing system in the world to continue using a pictorial form for over three thousand years. In fact it's the only major writing system in the world that has continued its pictograph-based development without interruption until modern times.

THE OFFICIAL AND NATIONAL LANGUAGE

The origins of Mandarin as the national language of China can be traced to the Manchu Qing Dynasty. For many centuries China's rulers faced a linguistic problem: in that vast land, people from different regions spoke many languages and dialects. In the seventeenth century, Qing Dynasty

The Chinese civilization was the first in the world to invent paper and printing. Recorded history shows that paper was first used in China in 105 CE and that printing was invented between 1041 and 1048, some three hundred years before it was first used in Europe.

officials encouraged the spread of the Peking dialect, which was the language used by government officials, called mandarins. Their success was limited.

In 1913, after the overthrow of the Manchu and the founding of the Republic of China, the government established a national standard of pronunciation based on the Peking dialect, with the aim of promoting a national language for China. Since then, Mandarin has been the national language of both the Republic of China on Taiwan and the People's Republic of China on the mainland. On the mainland, it is called *putonghua* (POO-tohng-hwa), meaning "common language."

Although Mandarin is the national tongue of the Taiwanese, its usage varies among the different groups of people. Mainlanders speak Mandarin most of the time, and, likewise, people who emigrated from mainland China after 1949—about 12 percent of the population—speak mainly Mandarin. Among the native Taiwanese (not aboriginals), who form about 84 percent of the population, Mandarin is spoken in offices and shops but not necessarily at home. About half of the native Taiwanese speak other Chinese dialects with their families. Many of the older generation of native Taiwanese, those born before 1940, may not speak Mandarin at all because they grew up during the Japanese occupation, when Japanese was taught in schools.

Geographical locations also play a part. Young people living or working in the northern parts of Taiwan typically speak Mandarin with their friends, whereas those in the southern areas tend to speak a mixture of Taiwanese, a dialect, and Mandarin.

Taiwanese Mandarin has been influenced by the dialects spoken on the island, especially the Fujian dialect. In fact, some Fujian words that have crept into Taiwanese Mandarin are so common, even the mainlanders use them.

COMING TO GRIPS WITH MANDARIN

The Chinese language is said to be one of the most complex languages in the world to learn. Not only are the sounds of the words difficult for a non-Chinese speaker to master, but writing it is an even more demanding task. Mandarin is a monosyllabic language, and this means that each syllable as pronounced has a unique meaning. Words may be made up of either one or more syllables. Considering that there are about four hundred syllables in the Chinese language, coming to grips with the full range of sounds can be daunting. Another characteristic of Mandarin is that it is a tonal language, in which there are several ways to pronounce each syllable. In fact, changing the tone of a particular character changes the meaning of that character, as in the examples below.

The four tones are:
- Constant (first tone), as in ma ̄ (mother)
- Rising (second tone), as in má (hemp)
- Falling and rising (third tone), as in ma ̌ (horse)
- Falling (fourth tone), as in mà (scold)

These four tonal variances add to the complexity of pronouncing Mandarin words. As each syllable can be pronounced in four ways, there are over 1,200 different syllables!

The language is structured on the subject-verb-object order that is similar to English. However, there are no past or present tenses, singular or plural configurations, or other grammatical rules. Writing in Chinese characters requires a great deal of memory work. The language is made up of about fifty thousand characters, although, to read a Chinese newspaper, the average person needs to know only about two thousand characters.

DIALECTS

The two most widely spoken dialects are the Fujian and Hakka dialects. Each is a form of the Chinese language peculiar to certain areas in China. The Fujian dialect comes from Fujian Province on the mainland. It is more commonly spoken in the southern part of Taiwan and in parts of the western coastal region that have historically absorbed immigrants from Fujian. Hakka originated from Hunan province on the mainland and is widely spoken in Taiwan's Hsin-chu, P'ing-tung, Miao-li, and T'ao-yüan counties, which have a sizable Hakka population.

In the 1960s and 1970s, Taiwan's official language policy was to place greater emphasis on Mandarin rather than the Chinese dialects. Now that Mandarin is firmly entrenched as the national language, there is greater

interest among the people in learning dialects. This revived interest over the past few years has resulted in the greater usage of dialects in the media. Since the late 1980s, existing television and radio programs in the Fujian and Hakka dialects have been expanded, and new programs have been introduced.

WRITTEN CHINESE

Many Chinese dialects are so far removed from each other that any spoken communication between them is a hit-

A calligrapher sells Chinese New Year's proverbs on red paper.

or-miss affair. Fortunately, there is a saving unifier in the written form of the language: all Chinese characters are written in exactly the same way regardless of dialect. So even if a government official from Peking is unable to communicate orally with someone from Fujian or Hunan province, they can communicate in writing. Chinese writing is based on ideograms—this means that each character is actually a pictorial representation of the idea being expressed.

Since 1964 the written form of Chinese in Taiwan and mainland China has taken different paths. Believing that standard Chinese characters were too complex for the average person to master, the Chinese Communists on the mainland introduced a simplified form of Chinese characters called *jiantizi* (JIAN ti tze). Taiwan, on the other hand, still retains the classical form of characters, called *fantizi* (FAHN ti tze).

ROMANIZATION

Since a large part of the world does not use Chinese characters, there have been many systems devised to Romanize the language—that is, to use the Latin alphabet to write in Chinese. Hanyu Pinyin has been the international standard since 1982.

The People's Republic of China adopted the system as far back as 1958, but Taiwan balked. In 2002, Taiwan chose to use Tongyong Pinyin, a variation as its official Romanization system. However, the issue quickly became a political one, with Romanization preferences reflecting issues of national identity.

The Kuomintang (Nationalists) and other pan-blue parties advocated the adoption of Hanyu Pinyin, in order to be on the same page with the mainland and much of the world. The Democratic Progressive and other pan-green parties favored the continuation of Tongyong Pinyin as a matter of national individuality and separateness from the mainland.

Although the matter was finalized in 2009 with the official switch to Hanyu Pinyin, many street signs and other public spellings still retain the old style, or—adding to the confusion—even older Romanization styles. In some cases, where the old-style spelling is universally recognized, such as in the spelling of the capital city Taipei, the old style has been retained. In Hanyu Pinyin, for example, the capital city's name would be Taibei.

NEWSPAPERS

Not long ago, Taiwan's newspapers were subject to a very restrictive policy that effectively imposed censorship. From the early 1950s until 1988, the KMT did not allow any new newspaper to publish and even restricted the number of pages in each issue. In 1955, newspapers were allowed to run eight pages of news only; that number was increased to twelve in 1974 and to thirty-two (or even forty) pages at a later stage.

In 1988, this restrictive policy was finally lifted, and as a result, many new newspapers have since been published. There are some 360 privately owned newspapers and numerous radio stations. Satellite TV systems carry more than 280 channels. The internet is not restricted by the government; about 84 percent of the population accessed the medium as of 2014.

Indeed, Taiwan's respect for press freedom was recognized in 2015 in a finding by Freedom House, which said, "Taiwan's media environment is one of the freest in Asia, and the vigorous and diverse press reports aggressively on government policies and alleged official wrongdoing." In fact, to keep the

CALLIGRAPHY

Calligraphy, or the art of writing, has been an important part of Chinese linguistic and artistic history for more than two thousand years. Because Chinese characters lend themselves to artistic interpretation, calligraphy is considered a cultural refinement. To a calligrapher a dot, for example, is full of life, and a line may burst with energy. Like the branch of a tree or a thick vine, there is logic to the form and behavior of each stroke.

Many calligraphic works are written on scrolls that are often hung in homes, offices, shops, and at monuments. These contain fragments of poems or the sayings of famous people. Different writing styles have evolved over the centuries, including the seal script, official script, regular script, running script, and cursive script.

The "four treasures of study" essential to calligraphy are the brush pen, paper, ink stick, and inkstone. These are the tools with which Chinese characters are written in the traditional way. Brush pens are made from soft, fine, animal hair and date back three thousand years. The earliest form of calligraphy (sixteenth–eleventh centuries BCE) was written on stones, tortoise shells, animal hides, and bones. Ever since the Chinese invented paper during the Eastern Han Dynasty (25–220 CE), calligraphy has been written on paper. Today, calligraphy is an important subject taught in schools in Taiwan.

media free of political influence, a law passed in 2003 prohibits government and political party officials from holding positions in broadcast media companies. Government and political parties had to divest themselves of all broadcasting assets.

Cyberattacks, however, pose a significant threat to Taiwan's freedom of the press. Cyberwarfare units on the Chinese mainland have been increasingly attacking Taiwanese media sites. News sites that criticize the Chinese government have found their websites going black at critical times, with the outage sometimes lasting for weeks.

INTERNET LINKS

freedomhouse.org/report/freedom-press/2015/taiwan
Freedom House evaluates Taiwan's freedoms of speech and press.

translate.google.com
Google Translate accommodates both Chinese characters and pinyin in translations to English.

www.omniglot.com/chinese/mandarin.htm
This introduction to Mandarin also includes information about pinyin.

www.omniglot.com/chinese/taiwanese.htm
Omniglot offers a good introduction to the Taiwanese (not Mandarin) language.

www.pinyin.info/romanization/tongyong/basic.html
This chart compares the syllables of Mandarin Chinese as written in both Tongyong and Hanyu Pinyin.

www.purpleculture.net/chinese-pinyin-converter
This online translator converts Chinese characters to pinyin.

ARTS

A colorful temple roof ornament displays the rich art of Taiwanese culture.

10

I N 2016, TAIPEI CITY WAS THE WORLD Design Capital, a title bestowed upon it by the International Council of Societies of Industrial Design, a nonprofit organization based in Montreal, Canada. For its banner year, Taipei staged a series of major arts and design events aimed at highlighting its reputation as a center of creativity and innovation.

If Taipei's design sector is on the cutting edge of what's new, Taiwan as a whole is likewise very much a twenty-first century arts scene. However, it's also a showcase for the rich artistic and cultural traditions of Chinese and aboriginal civilizations.

FINE ARTS

Calligraphy and painting form the basis of Chinese fine arts. Traditional Chinese painting uses ink and watercolors rather than oil-based paints. Landscapes and scenes from nature, such as animals and trees, are the most popular subjects, but many modern painters are experimenting with new artistic forms and Western-influenced artistic media.

Carving in stone, wood, or bamboo is a respected craft. Stone carvings are usually found in temples. Just about every temple has a pair of carved stone lions at the entrance, and carvings of dragons decorate the columns of temples. Wood carvings, both miniature and large, are generally made of sandalwood or camphor wood. One of Taiwan's most

One of Ju Ming's outdoor sculptures from The Living World series features businessmen with umbrellas.

famous contemporary artists and sculptors is Ju Ming (b. 1938). He has won international awards for his dramatic outdoor sculptures that give traditional Chinese subjects a modern look. For thirty years, he has been expanding on a particular project, the Living World series. These colorful sculptures depict people of all kinds engaged in ordinary activities; they are at once fantastical and mundane, humorous, serious, and profoundly perceptive.

Chinese pottery and porcelain have been famous around the world since the Ming Dynasty. Taiwan continues to produce the traditional blue and white ceramics for which Chinese potters are famous, as well as modern designs.

FOLK ARTS

Taiwan's diverse folk arts are part of its traditional culture. Many of the crafts evolved to celebrate the agricultural seasons, festivals, and major days in people's lives, such as birthdays, marriages, and deaths.

Paper cutting is one of the oldest folk arts. Red paper cutouts are pasted onto walls and windows to give homes a festive look. Knotting, or macramé, is used to make jewelry or wall hangings. During the Qing Dynasty (1644—1911) silk macramé decorated clothing, fans, ceremonial flutes, window shades, jade scepters, and many other items. One traditional craft of the Hakka people is the making of oilpaper umbrellas. The Hakkas in the town of Meinung in southern Taiwan are well known for this specialty.

Just about every festive event in Taiwan features a dazzling display of lion and dragon dances, the origins of which can be traced back to ancient China. Dragons, in particular, symbolize power and good fortune. Lion dances are performed in religious ceremonies and for entertainment. The dance is performed by two people. One carries the lion's head and leads the dance while the other plays the lion's body. The performers dance to the loud and stirring rhythm of drums, gongs, and cymbals. Another folk art that is a favorite with children is that of candy and rice-dough sculptures. Candies made of sugar and rice dough are molded into colorful animal and human shapes and sprinkled with sugar. The skill and detail that go into creating them qualify them as folk art.

Shadow puppets are a Chinese art form from the seventeenth century.

Taiwan's puppet theater has three forms—hand puppets, shadow puppets, and marionettes. These used to be an important part of many festivals and religious occasions but are now less popular among the people. The plots of puppet shows are usually based on myths, folk stories, and historical events. Some of these shows are broadcast on television.

There has been increasing concern in Taiwan that modern and Western influences may affect its folk art heritage. The annual four-day Lukang Folk Arts Festival aims to preserve Taiwan's unique art forms by promoting greater appreciation of them. Among the arts exhibited at the festival are lantern making, top spinning, candy and dough sculpting, paper cutting and folding, kite flying, carving, and puppetry. Dragon and lion dances, stilt walking, and music and dance performances keep audiences entertained and add to the festive atmosphere.

*A girl plays
a guzheng.*

MUSICAL TRADITION

Taiwan's music culture falls roughly into three broad categories—indigenous, Han Chinese, and Western. The folk music of the indigenous people often involves singing and dancing, especially during festivals and rituals, sometimes to the accompaniment of simple native instruments. Different ethnic groups have different musical traditions, however. The Bunun people don't dance much, but are best known for eight-part harmonic chant and song. Their instruments include five-string zithers and jaw harps.

Han Chinese music is rooted in the traditions of mainland China and is the most ancient musical style in all of Chinese society. Taiwan has three professional orchestras that perform classical music—the Taipei Municipal Orchestra, the Experimental Chinese Orchestra of the National Taiwan Academy of Arts, and the Chinese Music Orchestra of the Broadcasting Corporation of China. There are also over two hundred amateur and school orchestras. Many schools have classes teaching the use of traditional Chinese musical instruments.

Traditional musical instruments fall into four basic categories—those that can be blown, bowed, plucked, or struck. These include the *erhu* (ER-hoo), a two-stringed fiddle, the *yueqin* (YOO-eh chin), a four-stringed mandolin, the *guzheng* (KOO-chuhng), a zither, and the *pipa* (PEE-pah), a four-stringed lute. Other traditional instruments, such as trumpets and gongs, are used mainly in religious ceremonies in temples and at funerals. Interest in traditional Chinese music has suffered a decline as more people of present-day Taiwan prefer listening to contemporary pop and rock music.

TAIWANESE OPERA

Taiwanese opera is an offshoot of Peking opera, the most famous of Chinese dramatic forms. It is performed in the Fujian dialect and was brought to

Taiwan by the early immigrants. The opera owes its popularity to the artistic flowering that took place in mainland China in the Tang Dynasty (618—907 CE), and certain Tang emperors are considered "the honorary fathers of Chinese opera" for their support of opera.

Most Taiwanese operas are performed in the open air on a simple stage with only a backdrop. Hardly any props are used because the performers' costumes and gestures are so pictorial in themselves. Traditionally, the women's roles were played by men, but women now perform in modern operas. Each character has distinguishable costumes and fantastic facial makeup so that the audience can tell at a glance whom each player represents. Costumes worn in operas are based on those of the Ming Dynasty over four hundred years ago. Most operas tell stories of great historical events or folklore. A typical opera performance has dramatic swordfights between rivals, lovers' meetings, family disputes, and scenes of heartbreak and heroism.

Facial makeup in Taiwanese opera, an art in itself, is an outward representation of a character's personality. The origins of this form of makeup go back almost 1,500 years. In the sixth century CE, Prince Lan-ling of the Northern Wei kingdom tried to make himself look more fearsome in battle by painting an aggressive mask on his face. The strategy worked, and his enemies were so intimidated that they lost the battle, even though they had superior forces. Later, in the Tang dynasty, facial makeup was used in opera performances.

Today, different colors are used to symbolize different personalities. For instance, red indicates good character, white is for craftiness, blue represents bravery, black is for honesty, yellow signifies intelligence, brown suggests a strong personality, green is for ghosts or demons, and gold is for gods or good spirits.

CHINESE DANCE

In ancient times, music and dance were purely for rituals. With the passage of time, however, their function evolved into one of entertainment. Traditional Chinese dance has been divided into civilian and military dances for almost three thousand years. Civilian dance has more free-flowing

ANG LEE, RENOWNED FILM DIRECTOR

One of the most admired and successful movie directors in the world is Taiwan-born Ang Lee (b. 1954). His parents left mainland China in 1949 after the defeat of the Chinese Nationalists in the Civil War. He attended art school in Taiwan and went to the United States in 1979 to study theater. He was originally interested in acting, but because his English was heavily accented, he went into directing instead. Lee's first big hits were in Mandarin. The Wedding Banquet *(1993) and* Eat Drink Man Woman *(1995) brought him international acclaim and Academy Award nominations for Best Foreign Language Film.*

From that, Lee went to Hollywood and began making English language films. His big breakthrough came with Crouching Tiger, Hidden Dragon *(2000), a martial arts movie with an international crew. With Mandarin dialogue and English subtitles, the film was a surprising smash that won many awards. Lee went way out of his comfort zone with the Wyoming-based* Brokeback Mountain *(2005), for which he won his first Oscar as Best Director. He won it again for* Life of Pi *(2012).*

In 2006, Lee was awarded the Order of Brilliant Star with Grand Cordon by the Taiwanese government, the country's second highest civilian honor. Meanwhile, Lee is now a naturalized US citizen and lives in New York. His most recent movie is the war comedy, Billy Lynn's Long Halftime Walk, *set to open in November 2016.*

movements. Military dancers traditionally perform in large groups with coordinated movements.

A famous traditional dance in Taiwan is the Eight Rows Dance performed in temples every year during Confucius's birthday celebrations. Sixty-four young boys dressed in yellow robes are arranged in eight rows. Carrying pheasant tails and red batons, the boys bow, turn, and kneel in performing this stately dance that has remained unchanged since the Sung Dynasty (960—1279 CE).

Taiwan is experiencing a revival of interest in dance, especially those with techniques that combine traditional and modern dance elements. Among the troupes that have won acclaim for their blending of Chinese dance techniques with modern dance choreography are the Cloud Gate Dance Troupe and the new Classical Dance Troupe.

ARCHITECTURAL STYLES IN TAIWAN

Because traditional Chinese society had large, extended families living together, typical Taiwanese homes were often big, rambling compounds that could house up to fifty family members. Most such homes consisted of one large central building with several wings or smaller buildings attached to it. The head of the family lived in the largest building, where the ancestral hall was also located. The hall held the family altar and portraits of deceased ancestors. The entire house, with its attached wings, was surrounded by a walled enclosure. Courtyards were important features of those homes because this was where the household chores were done. Another characteristic of this time-honored architecture is that buildings usually faced south. One possible reason for that could have been to avoid the harsh winds that blew down from the north.

A distinctive feature of Chinese architecture can be seen in the shape of roofs. In imperial China a person's social status was reflected in the roof of his home, and imperial court officials regulated the types of roofs people could build. Originally, only temples and government officials were allowed to have swallowtail roofs, where the ends of the roofs curved upward like a swallow's tail. Many wealthy families in Taiwan chose not to observe this

Taiwan's most prized collection of art treasures is housed in the famous National Palace Museum in Taipei. There are more than 620,000 priceless artifacts in this fabulous collection. Many artifacts in the museum are from the Chinese imperial collection that began in the Sung Dynasty over one thousand years ago. These were taken to Taiwan by the KMT, led by Chiang Kai-shek, when the party fled the Communist revolution on the mainland in 1949. During the Cultural Revolution in Communist China, many historical and art treasures were systematically destroyed as a result of government policy. Taiwan's collection of Chinese historical and art treasures is now one of the most extensive in the world.

mainland ruling and built their houses with swallowtail roofs. The Grand Hotel in Taipei is said to have the biggest classical swallowtail roof in the world. Ordinary people could build only horseback roofs that were rounded and shaped like a horse's back; these became characteristic of traditional farmhouses in Taiwan.

Modern architecture since the 1970s has increasingly been influenced by international architectural styles, and most apartment buildings in Taipei are very similar in style to those in Western countries. However, one important aspect of Chinese architecture that still has an impact on Taiwan's buildings is feng shui (FUHNG shway), or geomancy. Literally "wind and water," this is an Eastern practice based on the belief that nonliving objects can influence people's living environment. In accordance with feng shui, building construction in Taiwan follows certain fundamental principles. An important principle is that the front and back doors should not face each other directly in a straight line as this would allow good luck to pass right through and out of a building without stopping for a visit.

The Grand Hotel in Taipei displays typical Taiwanese style.

INTERNET LINKS

www.mofa.gov.tw/en/NewsNoHeadOnlyTitle. aspx?n=D63485FC2A6F4D3C&sms=CE9D6F5CD437EB7A
The Taiwan Ministry of Foreign Affairs presents a Culture and Lifestyle section with good articles about music, dance, calligraphy, architecture, opera, and puppetry.

www.npm.gov.tw/en
The National Palace Museum site has links to special sections with lovely videos, found under the Collections banner.

www.nytimes.com/movies/person/166472/Ang-Lee
This *New York Times* page has the scoop on director Ang Lee.

www.orientalarchitecture.com/taiwan/taipei
Asian Historical Architecture presents a slide show of Taipei's famous buildings.

www.taiwan.gov.tw/ct.asp?xItem=126578&CtNode=3774&mp=1
This Taiwan government site gives a good overview of the nation's arts scene.

LEISURE

A young girl enjoys a day in the park in Taipei.

11

WHEN IT COMES TO RELAXATION and recreation, the Taiwanese spend their free time in much the same way most people do. They enjoy time at home with family and friends, watch TV, surf the Internet, head to the mall, go to the movies, or grab a bite to eat. Kids play video games or, when their parents insist, which many do, use their time studying. One thing many people are not doing enough of, some health experts warn, is exercising. Obesity rates in Taiwan have been climbing steadily in recent years, and childhood obesity, now at 25 percent, is close to US levels. Diet is one part of the problem, but a sedentary lifestyle is as well.

Convenience stores are everywhere in Taiwan. The 7-Eleven chain is especially dominant; in 2014, it opened its five thousandth store in Taiwan. 7-Eleven's Taiwanese mascot, named Open-Chan, a cartoon dog with a rainbow on his head, is a national celebrity with his own music album and a theme park.

OUTINGS IN THE PARK

The park is a very important venue for leisure activities in Taiwan. Almost every day city parks are thronged with people walking, exercising, meditating, gossiping, or just relaxing. Weekends are even busier as whole families turn up to enjoy the fresh air and scenery.

Early morning is the best time to exercise in the park. This is when hundreds of people, young and old, head to the park to exercise before going to school or work. Among the different ways of working out are tai chi, dancing, calisthenics, and racket games, such as badminton. Among the older generation, it is common to see men playing Chinese chess in the park. Some even bring portable music players and hold singing sessions there.

OTHER ACTIVITIES

Besides spending time in the parks, many families eat out on Saturdays and Sundays or go shopping. Taipei's shopping malls are crowded with people, and night markets bustle with shoppers. Shilin Night Market is one of the largest night markets in Taipei, and the flower and jade markets also attract shoppers. Taipei's exotic Snake Alley bustles with buyers and the

The Shilin Night Market in Taipei is a famous attraction for shoppers.

curious—the marketplace sells everything from snakes to medicinal potions made from animal extracts.

Some families visit temples on Sundays, and other families visit the National Palace Museum, the zoo, or one of the many new amusement parks. Playing mahjong (MAH-johng) is popular with adults. Taiwanese teenagers go to the movies, meet their friends in parks, or hold barbeques. When it rains or is too cold, young people get together in amusement arcades to bowl or to play pool, table tennis, and computer games.

MARTIAL ARTS

Some forms of exercise that are unique to the Chinese are based on the martial arts. Tai chi chuan (TAI jee CHWAHN), or tai chi for short, is the ancient Chinese art of shadowboxing. It is actually a form of exercise with a series of set meditative movements, sometimes performed to music. The graceful movements exercise the muscles, enhance breathing, and are believed to stimulate the digestive and nervous systems. Chinese-style kung fu (KOONG foo) is also a popular martial art and forms part of the physical education curriculum in schools.

In Chinese kung fu a distinction is made between external and internal kung fu. In external kung fu the muscles, bones, and skin are exercised. In internal kung fu the spirit, mind, and internal life force are trained. The higher one's level of achievement in kung fu, the better one's ability to maintain good health and to live a long, active life.

The ideal time to practice tai chi or any other martial art is in the early morning, when chi, the life force or energy believed to be embodied in every living thing, is at its peak. Martial art displays can be seen daily in Taipei's city parks, at Sun Yat-sen Memorial Hall, and at Yang-ming-shan National Park.

Boys demonstrate martial arts techniques at the Burning King Boat Ceremony in Sikang, Taiwan.

For Taiwanese who are looking to get away from it all for a few days, leisure farms have become the new big thing. There are some two hundred recreational farms on the island, catering to weary urban visitors looking to commune with nature. The facilities range from rustic to sophisticated, and many were once —or still are—working farms. They offer beautiful scenery, wide-open spaces, animals, activities, and traditional arts and crafts in addition to overnight accommodations and meals.

Enjoying the farm-fresh foods produced and prepared on site is a special pleasure for guests. The Fairy Lake Leisure Farm in Tainan City, for example, is a 128-acre (52 ha) hilltop abode that grows tropical fruits such as longan, coffee litchi, ponkan oranges. Flying Cow Ranch in Miaoli County, one of the oldest leisure farms, is a dairy farm on almost 300 acres (120 ha). It has become a leading tourist

Flying Cow Ranch

attraction in Taiwan, particularly for families with children. The Shangri-La Leisure Farm, dramatically perched high up in mountain country, overlooking the ocean in Yilan County, is one of the best known of these resorts.

GETTING AWAY

Taiwan's dramatic mountain scenery offers city dwellers the opportunity to get away from the noise and stress of city life. Hiking in the Central Mountain Range has become a popular leisure pastime, and hiking clubs in Taiwan enjoy a growing popularity. Evergreen forests cover two-thirds of the island, and hikers can enjoy scenic views of forests, plains, waterfalls, and lakes.

Yü Shan National Park is a favorite destination of many. The largest and most pristine national park in Taiwan, Yü Shan offers hiking trails and showcases the ruins of aboriginal settlements and the Qing Dynasty. Another popular locale for enthusiastic hikers is Xueshan ("Snow Mountain"), the second highest mountain in Taiwan. Standing at an impressive height of 10,321 feet (3,146 m), Hehuan Shan ("Mountain of Harmonious Joy") in the Central Mountain Range is Taiwan's only ski resort. Besides drawing skiers in winter, it attracts numerous hikers during summer.

The Taiwanese also enjoy traveling to mountain resorts to take in the scenery. The tranquil beauty of Sun Moon Lake makes it a favorite destination among honeymooners and tourists. Ali Shan, with views of eighteen mountain peaks in the Central Mountain Range and the grand Taroko Gorge, also boasts a popular resort. A favorite excursion from Taipei involves a trip to the shore. The dramatic, rocky, coastal scenery of Yehliu in the northern part of the island draws many of Taipei's residents who like to visit the area on weekends.

The Central Mountains in Taiwan offer beautiful vistas.

SPORTS

The most popular sports in Taiwan are baseball, basketball, and table tennis. These games are played by children in schools and have a wide following among adults as well. Many Taiwanese also enjoy golf and tennis.

Baseball came to Taiwan during the years of Japanese rule. Boys and girls in elementary and junior high schools play baseball, and there are many Little Leagues and amateur teams. In 2001 Taiwan hosted the baseball World Cup and took a respectable third place. Baseball

A pitcher for the President Lions shows his form in a pro baseball game.

games are aired on television, and the Chinese Professional Baseball League is closely followed by fans every year. However, the league has been plagued by numerous gambling and game-fixing scandals—as recently as 2009—which has caused many teams to disband. Today there are only four teams in the league, the La New Bears, the Brother Elephants, the EDA Rhinos, and the Uni-President 7-Eleven Lions. Taiwan's best players often find higher-paying jobs with professional teams in Japan or the United States. The Chinese Taipei Baseball Team is the national team, which plays internationally and in the Olympics. This team is highly regarded and was ranked fourth in the world, behind Cuba, the United States, and Japan.

Basketball, introduced to Taiwan by Nationalist soldiers, attracted a large following until 1989, when Taipei's Chunghua Stadium burned down. It is enjoying a resurgence, and there are now two professional leagues.

TRADITIONAL SPORTS

Skipping with a jump rope has been popular since the Tang Dynasty and is promoted in calisthenics exercises in schools. Shuttlecock is described in historical records of the Han and Sung dynasties. The object is to kick a shuttlecock back and forth and keep it from falling to the ground. Top spinning became popular during the Sung Dynasty. Although the game was once popular with children, it is played mainly by men in Taiwan today. Diabolo spinning is taught in schools. The diabolo looks like a large yo-yo; it has two wooden or plastic wheels with a shaft between them. The player moves the diabolo by using a long cotton string attached to a stick at either end of the string.

KARAOKE

The Taiwanese love karaoke, or, as they call it, Karaoke Television (KTV). Singing along to prerecorded music videos is a popular activity for socializing. Karaoke is actually a Japanese word meaning "empty orchestra." Karaoke clubs offer private rooms with television sets, music videos, and a microphone. Many families have their own set up at home, where karoake is a favorite pastime on stormy days.

INTERNET LINKS

www.hardballtimes.com/professional-baseball-in-taiwan/#
This article looks at the state of professional baseball in Taiwan.

lifestyle.inquirer.net/176541/why-leisure-farms-in-taiwan-are-now-the-hot-destinations
The growing popularity of leisure farms is the topic of this article.

www.taipeitimes.com/News/feat/archives/2006/06/23/2003315209
This article explores the practice of martial arts in Taiwan.

FESTIVALS

New Year's fireworks light up the Taipei 101 building on January 1, 2014.

12

HOLIDAYS IN TAIWAN ARE A combination of traditional Chinese festivals, religious and government holidays, and aboriginal celebrations. The year kicks off with the Lunar New Year, which is not the same as the January 1 New Year of the Western calendar. However, January 1 is a special day because it is Foundation of the Republic of China Day, which marks the day that Sun Yat-sen was sworn in as the first president of Taiwan.

Many of the traditional Chinese holidays relate to the agricultural year. In times past, people were more dependent on the weather for their livelihood, and festivals marked the passing of the seasons. For example, the Lunar New Year falls in winter, when farmers cannot work in the fields, leaving them free time to celebrate. Tomb-Sweeping Day falls between the spring plowing and summer weeding, and the Mid-Autumn Festival is held around the final harvest of the year, when people can begin to relax. At festival celebrations different generations within a family reaffirm their bonds. They are occasions for rest and relaxation when people take time off from work and their busy lifestyles.

MAJOR NATIONAL HOLIDAYS

The Foundation of the Republic of China Day on January 1 is the anniversary of the date when Sun Yat-sen was sworn in as the first

Christmas is not celebrated much in Taiwan, and December 25 is Constitution Day. However, the secular and commercial aspects of Christmas are catching on there and it's not unusual to see Taiwanese-style Christmas decorations in the larger cities. As an unofficial holiday, however, Taiwan's Christmas is more of a romantic, Valentine's Day-type of affair.

FESTIVALS AND NATIONAL HOLIDAYS

Foundation of the Republic of China Day . . . . *January 1*

Lunar New Year . . . . *January/February (varies)*

Lantern Festival . . . . *first full moon of lunar year*

Peace Memorial Day . . . . *February 28*

Tomb-Sweeping Day. . . . . *April 5*

Labor Day . . . . *May 1*

Dragon Boat Festival . . . . *5th day of 5th lunar month (usually June)*

Ghost Month. . . . . *7th lunar month (August/September)*

Confucius's Birthday. . . . . *September 28*

Moon Festival . . . . *15th day of 8th lunar month (September/October)*

Double Ten or National Day . . . . *October 10*

Retrocession Day. . . . . *October 25*

Chiang Kai-shek's Birthday . . . . *October 31*

Sun Yat-sen's Birthday. . . . . *November 12*

Constitution Day . . . . *December 25*

president of the Republic of China. Double Ten Day, or National Day, on October 10 (10/10) marks the fall of the Qing Dynasty and the establishment of the Republic of China. Double Ten is the most colorful of all the secular holidays. This is the occasion for huge rallies, parades with lion and dragon dances, and displays of martial arts, acrobatics, and folk dances. The grand finale is a splendid fireworks display.

Retrocession Day on October 25 is the anniversary of the day in 1945 when the Japanese occupation of Taiwan ended and the island returned to Chinese rule. The birthdays of two important historic figures in the Republic of China's history are also celebrated: Sun Yat-sen's birthday on November 12, and Chiang Kai-shek's birthday on October 31. Constitution Day on December 25 commemorates the day in 1947 when the constitution of the Republic of China on Taiwan came into force.

LUNAR NEW YEAR

The Lunar New Year, or Chinese New Year, is the single most important festival of every Chinese community anywhere in the world. It usually falls in late January or early February, depending on variations in the lunar calendar. The festival actually lasts for fifteen days, but only New Year's Eve and the first two days are public holidays in Taiwan. However, most offices and shops close during the first week of the Lunar New Year.

Chinese New Year's decorations carry lucky symbols.

The weeks leading up to the new year are a busy time for most people. To make sure they get off to a good start in the year ahead, people stock up on food, buy new clothes, spring-clean, and decorate their houses with Chinese characters inviting good luck.

One of the highlights of this festival is the traditional family reunion dinner. On the eve of the Lunar New Year, family members, who may be living far away, return to their parents' home to share in a lavish dinner. The children have a great time. They are given "lucky money" in red envelopes, or *hung bao*. Families relax after dinner, catch up on the local gossip, and stay up through the night to welcome the New Year. Finally fireworks are set off to frighten away evil spirits.

The second day of the Lunar New Year is when family members remember their ancestors and offer sacrifices. Ritual offerings are made to ancestors at the family shrine, followed by offerings to the gods at temples, with prayers asking for a happy and prosperous year. Family members also visit each other with the traditional greeting of "*Kung hsi fa tsai!*" (KOHNG see fah TSAI), meaning "Congratulations! Get rich!" or "Good luck and prosperity!" People stay at home on the third day because this is when bad luck is believed to be in the air. The next few days are a time of increased activity: firecrackers are set off to welcome the gods, offerings are made to them, and sacrificial money is burned.

On the fifteenth day of the Lunar New Year, the Lantern Festival (Yuan Xiao) traditionally marks the end of the special days. This is a fascinating celebration of its own, and is an especially happy time for children, who play a major role in this part of the festival.

The ancient Chinese believed that celestial spirits could be seen in the first full moon of the lunar year, and people lit lanterns to see the spirits. Today, children carry on this tradition in temples, parks, and streets all over Taiwan. The lanterns are usually red to symbolize good fortune.

The most glorious lantern celebration in Taiwan is the Pingxi Sky Lantern Festival, which originated in the mountain town of Pingxi, but which now tours the country. Typically, up to two hundred thousand candle-lit paper lanterns are launched into the full moonlit evening sky, each carrying the hand-written desires of the person who launched it. The phenomenon is a luminous sight to behold.

Throughout Taiwan, as well as China, people eat glutinous rice balls called tangyuan *or* yuanxiao *at this time. The dumplings, which can be sweet or savory, are round to symbolize the full moon and the unity of the family. In Taiwanese society, where age is looked upon with great respect, there is a common saying that people will not gain a year in age until they eat a tangyuan.*

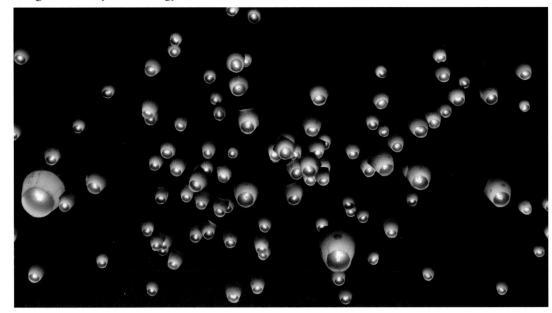

The sixth day is the birthday of the god Tsu Shih, and the seventh day is celebrated as the anniversary of the creation of human beings. The ninth day is another day for making offerings as it is the birthday of the Jade Emperor, the supreme deity of the Taoist religion.

TOMB-SWEEPING DAY

Tomb-Sweeping Day is observed on April 5, which is also the anniversary of the death of President Chiang Kai-shek. This day is an important ancestral festival when the Taiwanese remember their deceased family members. Entire families visit the graves of their ancestors and offer prayers to them. The graves are swept free of dirt, and fresh flowers and offerings of food and wine are placed in front of the tombs. The ceremony must be performed before dawn or in the early morning because it is necessary that the spirits of the departed, who sleep during the night, still be "at home" in their tombs.

People pay their respects to their ancestors on Tomb-Sweeping Day.

The Taiwanese believe they fulfill their obligation of filial respect and please their ancestors by remembering them on Tomb-Sweeping Day. A poem from the Tang Dynasty describes the intense emotional bond living people feel for their departed ancestors:

> *On Tomb-Sweeping Day as the rain falls everywhere, people walking in the streets feel the sorrow within and without.*

DRAGON BOAT FESTIVAL

Also called the Double Fifth Festival, because it falls on the fifth day of the fifth lunar month—typically in June—the Dragon Boat Festival is one of the most important holidays. It commemorates the death of Qu Yuan, a scholar-statesman of the Warring States period (475—221 BCE) during the

Boats race in the Love River during the 2015 Dragon Boat Festival in Kaosiung.

Zhou Dynasty, who drowned himself in a river in protest against tyranny and corruption. The legend is that upon his death, those who respected his honesty and sacrifice went out in boats to search for his body. When they could not find it, they threw cooked rice into the river so that the fish would not eat Qu Yuan's body.

Teams take part in dragon boat races to commemorate the search for Qu Yuan. The most famous race today is the one in Taipei, where teams from all over the country vie for the Chiang Kai-shek Memorial Cup. Dragon boats are colorfully decorated with elaborate dragon heads. They are about 43 feet (13 m) long and have a helmsman, a drummer, eighteen to twenty-two oarsmen, and a flag catcher. Women's dragon boat races use smaller boats.

Another custom is the eating of *zongzi* (JONG tze), a rice dumpling stuffed with pork or beans. This is in memory of the people who threw rice into the river to keep the fish from eating Qu Yuan's body.

GHOST MONTH

The Chinese believe that the ghosts of the dead return to Earth for a visit during the seventh lunar month. To appease these spirits and prevent them from causing harm, the Taiwanese offer prayers, food, wine, and burn sacrificial paper money. Both Buddhist and Taoist priests perform prayer rites in their temples every day during this month. Lanterns are hung on bamboo poles in temple courtyards to invite the ghosts to enter and listen to the prayers offered to them. It is regarded as inauspicious to conduct weddings and new business ventures during this month. People also avoid surgery, buying cars, swimming, and going out after dark.

MOON FESTIVAL

Originally called the Mid-Autumn Festival, this major holiday celebrates the appearance of the biggest and brightest full moon of the year, which coincides with the end of the harvest, in September or October. The Taiwanese make a family event of this festival. Typically, all members of the family will go to parks to gaze at "the Lady in the Moon" and to eat mooncakes. It is believed that the Lady in the Moon was once the wife of a Tang emperor. She drank a magic potion and flew up to the moon, where she has been ever since.

Mooncakes are a festive holiday treat.

Mooncakes are round pastries stuffed with sweet bean paste. They have a historical symbolism for the Chinese, being a reminder of the time during the Yuan Dynasty (1280—1368) when China was ruled by the Mongols. To overthrow the Mongols, people had to rally enough support to start a rebellion, and messages hidden in mooncakes were passed around for this purpose.

ABORIGINAL FESTIVALS

Aboriginal festivals are colorful occasions celebrated with a great sense of ceremony and pageantry. Many aborigines who have moved to the cities and assimilated with the Chinese make a point of returning to their home villages to celebrate various festivals.

HARVEST FESTIVAL The Harvest Festival celebrated by the Ami is one of the most important aboriginal festivals. It lasts for seven days in late summer, at the end of the harvest season. During the first three days of the festival people sit down to talk about what they have achieved in the past year. This is followed by singing and dancing in the village square.

During this time the Ami also have a Proposal Festival for the unmarried. Young people spend time together to get acquainted, and on the last night of the Harvest Festival, a young woman chooses the man she wants to get engaged to by obtaining his belt. A chosen man then sends twenty bundles of firewood to the woman's family; if these are accepted, the engagement becomes official.

FLYING FISH FESTIVAL This festival, which is observed by the Yami, is based on an ancient myth about a talking fish that taught the tribe to follow a strict set of rules concerning the catching and eating of fish. According to legend, two Yami fishermen caught a huge winged fish that could fly. A little later, the fishermen's families found sores breaking out on their skin. The tribal elder then had a dream about a fish called Blackfin, who asked to meet him the next day. Blackfin actually appeared before the old man the next day and taught him the rituals and ceremonies associated with the fishing season and the catching of flying fish.

To this day, the Yami observe these rituals. At the start of the flying fish season, they destroy old fish-drying racks and build new ones, and put new fences around each house. The Yami men put on ceremonial dress with silver caps and beautiful jewelry and go out to sea in decorated boats to catch flying fish. These fish are considered to be special and are not cooked in the same pots as other fish. On the day itself, people allow no strangers to visit.

FESTIVAL OF THE LITTLE PEOPLE The origin of this Saisiyat festival is told in a story dating back five hundred years. At the time, the Saisiyat were not good farmers, but they managed to learn farming techniques from a group of pygmies. Unfortunately, the two peoples quarreled, and the Saisiyat killed the pygmies. After that, the Saisiyat became afraid that the spirits of the pygmies would take revenge, so they held a festival to appease and exorcise the spirits.

The theme of this festival still lies in appeasing the pygmy spirits through song and dance. The spirits are invited to attend the festival with ritual singing and dancing that lasts the whole night. Over the next few days the pygmy spirits are greeted and entertained with more traditional songs and dances. On the seventh and last day, a small tree is placed over the spirit shrine. Young Saisiyat men then proceed to exorcise the spirits by throwing pieces of the tree at the eastern sky and by staging an aggressive dance to frighten away the spirits.

INTERNET LINKS

www.fest300.com/festivals/pingxi-sky-lantern-festival
See a slideshow of images of the Pingxi Sky Lantern Festival on this site.

go2taiwan.net/monthly_selection.php?sqno=21
"Aboriginal Tribes & Festivals" is one of many informative pages on this site.

www.roughguides.com/destinations/asia/taiwan/festivals-public-holidays
This site offers an overview of major and minor Taiwanese celebrations.

www.travelking.com.tw/eng/tourguide/taiwanfestivals
This travel site has some good images and explanations of the major Taiwan holidays.

FOOD

Young green rice grows in a paddy.

13

C HINESE FOOD IS SO POPULAR that Chinese restaurants can be found almost everywhere—in most international cities and in plenty of small towns as well. Indeed, authentic Chinese cookery—which isn't necessarily what is served at the average take-out joint— is acknowledged to be one of the most refined and sophisticated cuisines in the world. So it may be surprising to learn that Taiwanese cuisine is relatively unknown— outside of Taiwan, that is.

As in other parts of Asia, rice or *fan* (fahn) is the most important staple, especially for the Taiwanese who migrated from southern China. In just about every meal, dishes of meat and vegetables are eaten with rice. Many food products are also made from rice. There are rice cakes, rice noodles, rice congee (porridge), and rice wine. In fact, eating and rice are such a central part of the Chinese culture that many conversations begin with the heartwarming greeting, "*Chi fan le mei you*?" (CHUH fahn luh may yoh), meaning "Have you eaten rice?" or "Have you had your meal?" Chinese cooking is also famous for its noodles, although noodles are mainly a feature of northern Chinese food.

The Chinese have long held a traditional belief in the medicinal value of food. Many plants used in Chinese cooking, such as scallions, ginger, garlic, dried lily buds, and tree fungus, are believed to have properties of preventing or alleviating various illnesses.

COOKING STYLES

Tea-smoked duck breast is a favorite Szechuan dish.

As immigrants from the mainland settled in Taiwan over the centuries, they took with them cuisines from different parts of mainland China. In a country as vast as China, many regions have evolved their own styles of cooking, and these styles are named after the regions in which they first originated.

The Szechuan style, with its hot and spicy dishes originating from Szechuan Province, is one of the most popular cooking styles in Taiwan. A famous Szechuan dish is camphor- and tea-smoked duck. The duck is marinated in a flavoring of ginger, cinnamon, peppercorns, orange peel, and coriander, and then steamed. What gives this dish its distinctive flavor and name is the next stage, when the duck is smoked over a charcoal fire made aromatic with tea leaves and camphor wood.

Hunanese food from Hunan Province is hot and spicy or sweet and sour. Honey ham and frogs' legs in chili sauce are specialties of this province. Beggar's chicken, a well-known dish in Taiwan, is also of Hunanese origin. According to legend, there was once a poor man who stole a chicken. When he saw some guards approaching, he covered the chicken with mud and threw it into a fire. After the guards had left, the man cracked open the dried mud and found a fragrant cooked chicken.

Hakka food, also from Hunan province, is simple, country-style fare. There are no fancy sauces, and the dishes are mostly pork-based.

Szechuan and Hunanese food represent the western Chinese style of cooking. Northern cuisine is seen in the Peking and Mongolian cooking styles. Peking cuisine features more wheat-based food and less rice. Lamb is a part of its menu. Mongolian barbecues, where meat and vegetables are grilled on a large hot plate, are very popular in Taiwan.

Cantonese food from southern China is bland in comparison with other styles as it has minimal flavoring. Most dishes are stir-fried or steamed. Cantonese food is perhaps the best known Chinese food in the West because most Chinese immigrants to Europe and America were Cantonese and cooked in the Cantonese style when they set up restaurants.

The eastern style of cooking is seen in Shanghainese food, another popular cuisine in Taiwan. This usually features rich and slightly sweet sauces and is well known for its range of seafood dishes. Taiwanese food is indigenous to Taiwan. It is similar to Shanghainese food in that it features a lot of seafood and uses the same seasonings. It also uses lots of seafood, as well as taro, radishes, and sweet potatoes—all of which grow well in Taiwan. Popular dishes are salted radish omelet and three-cups chicken (which can also be made with frog). Three-cups dishes are made with soy sauce, rice wine, and sesame oil—all measured out in cups. Recipes today, however, use less oil. In night markets, many Taiwanese enjoy another traditional Taiwanese snack—the oyster omelet.

Three-cups chicken, a popular Taiwanese dish is flavored with garlic, ginger, and basil.

MEALS AND MEALTIMES

Traditional Chinese breakfasts usually include bread, eggs, and milk—but with a difference. The bread is not Western-style bread but rather consists of traditional steamed rolls or deep-fried dough sticks called *you tiao* (YOO ti-ow), and milk is not dairy milk but soybean milk. Fried eggs usually accompany these. Another breakfast dish is congee, a rice porridge with a savory fish, chicken, or pork flavoring. The Taiwanese place great importance on having at least a light meal each morning, so it is not common to skip breakfast. However, breakfast tends to be a quick meal for family members who have to rush off to work or school.

For most working people, lunch is also a quick meal. Some people pack a lunch box of rice with some meat and vegetables, but many others eat at outdoor food stalls or restaurants that cater to the lunchtime crowd. In most homes the Taiwanese tend to have dinner between 6 and 7 pm when family members return from work. Dinner usually consists of a hot soup, rice or

Deep fried bread sticks with coconut jam make a quick breakfast.

Tea drinking is an important cultural and gastronomic institution in Taiwan. It is polite and sociable to invite someone to have tea, so every visitor is automatically offered a cup of cha (chah), or tea.

Tea is made from tea leaves that are treated in different ways. Green tea is made from unfermented leaves; black tea is fully fermented and has an aroma of malt; and oolong tea, or "black dragon tea," is partially fermented. Other teas are made from blends of tea leaves and flowers, such as jasmine and chrysanthemum. Tea is one of Taiwan's agricultural products that grows best in a subtropical climate at a high elevation.

Chinese tea is made by pouring boiling water onto tea leaves and leaving this to steep for a few minutes. No milk or sugar is added, so all one tastes is the flavor of the tea. A certain ritual is attached to brewing tea. First, a small teapot, ideally made of copper-colored pottery, is warmed by pouring boiling water into it. This water is then discarded. Fresh boiling water is again poured into the teapot and tea leaves added, but the first brew of the tea is not drunk. It is poured away instead. Tea and boiling water are then placed into the teapot a second time and left to steep for a minute or two. It is only then that the tea is poured into little cups to be drunk. The flaky tea leaves are not strained but left to float on top. Since the leaves are bitter, people avoid swallowing them by holding up the cup and blowing gently on the tea. This pushes the leaves away so that they can sip the tea without taking in the leaves.

Tea drinking is an important national institution. This is reflected in the number of tea houses where people meet to drink tea, munch on snacks, read, relax, and even conduct business. The culture of tea drinking is so strong that it has spawned a variety of savory snacks to go with it. The snacks are called yum cha *(YAHM chah) in Taiwan. They are actually a Cantonese invention known in the West as* dim sum *(DIM sum, a Cantonese term) and in China as* tien hsin *(DEE-yen sin). Tea snacks are believed to have originated six hundred years ago during the Yuan Dynasty.*

noodles, and two or three other dishes of meat or seafood and vegetables. Desserts are not featured widely in Chinese meals, particularly at home, but fruit is normally eaten after dinner, as the Taiwanese believe this helps digestion and clears the palate.

EATING OUT

The eating habits of Taiwanese people have been affected, to some degree, by modern urban living. Hence, while it used to be

Vendors prepare food offerings at the Kenting night market.

the case that most Taiwanese would eat at home most of the time, many urban-dwelling, working Taiwanese eat out quite a lot nowadays and often in informal, family-style stalls and eateries. Whether at home or in a restaurant, the Taiwanese observe traditional etiquette associated with eating. For example, meals must be eaten while seated, and there is a particular order to who may be seated first among the men and women, young and old. Meals are served at round tables, and each table can usually seat up to ten or twelve people. At restaurants the host usually places the orders, but it is considered polite for the host to ask guests to suggest dishes. The meal usually starts with a cold dish of appetizers. Dishes are brought in course after course. They are placed in the center of the table on a rotating turntable and everyone helps themselves to a little of each dish. Dining etiquette demands that one selects pieces of food closest to one and not stretch for a choice bit. The main courses are eaten with chopsticks, and soup is sipped from a spoon. The last dish is usually a plate of fried rice or noodles.

At dinner parties, toasts are often exchanged. There is a particular ritual and etiquette to making toasts—it is considered polite to hold the glass with one hand and to have the other hand touching the base of the glass. The host usually makes a toast at the beginning of the meal by saying "*kan pei*" (GAHN bay), meaning "bottoms up." If the person making the toast says "*suei yi*" (SWAY yi), meaning "as you please," the others present may either take a sip of their drink or drink up completely—as they please.

YIN AND YANG FOOD

The Chinese believe that all types of food can be categorized into three basic types. Hot, or *yang* (yahng), food heats the blood and reduces vital energy, whereas cold, or yin, food cools the blood and increases vital energy. Neutral, or ping, foods are balanced and do not affect energy either way.

Yang foods are usually favored in winter, when the blood needs to be warmed, and cooling yin foods beat the heat of summer. When ordering meals in restaurants, the Taiwanese aim to achieve a balance of all three types of food—fried foods are yang and are balanced with steamed, or yin, foods; meat dishes (yang) are balanced with vegetables (yin); and yang spices are balanced with yin fruits.

INTERNET LINKS

www.cnn.com/2015/07/23/travel/40-taiwan-food
This is a slideshow of forty Taiwanese dishes.

www.eatingchina.com/recipes.htm
The Chinese recipes on this site are mostly from Taiwan.

www.laweekly.com/restaurants/10-classic-taiwanese-dishes-2376671
This page shows large photos of ten popular Taiwanese foods.

www.tastespotting.com/tag/Taiwanese
This is a portal to some in depth reviews, photos and recipes for Taiwanese cuisine.

NIU ROU MIAN (TAIWANESE BEEF NOODLE SOUP)

This soup is often called Taiwan's national dish.

2 pounds (900 grams) stew beef, preferably boneless beef shank
1 tablespoon vegetable oil
5 cloves of garlic, smashed
1 inch chunk of ginger, sliced
2 Thai chilies, split lengthwise
2 star anise
2 scallions, chopped
2 Tbsp chili bean sauce
½ cup (120 milliliters) soy sauce
1 tomato, sliced
½ cup (120 mL) rice wine
2 Tbsp sugar
1 Tbsp Sichuan peppercorns
1 teaspoon five-spice powder
2 lbs (900 g) Asian noodles
hot sauce

Heat oil in large soup pot or Dutch oven. Working in batches, brown meat over medium high heat, turning, until all pieces are browned. Transfer meat to another dish and set aside.

Over medium heat, sauté garlic, ginger, scallions, chilies, and star anise in oil until fragrant, about 3 or 4 minutes. Return beef to pot, add chili bean sauce. Add rice wine and cook for 2 minutes. Add tomato, soy sauce, and sugar. Add water and remaining spices until everything is just covered. Bring to medium high heat and then reduce to a simmer for about 3 hours, or until the beef is very tender. Add hot sauce to taste.

Cook noodles according to package directions, drain. Divide among individual soup bowls. Ladle soup into each bowl along with chunks of beef. Top with chopped scallions. Serves 6 to 8.

CHA YE DAN (TEA EGGS)

These pretty eggs are a popular snack in Taiwan.

1 dozen hard boiled eggs,
  cooled
2 tea bags (black tea)
¼ cup (60 mL) soy sauce
1 star anise

Lightly crack the shell of each egg by gently tapping on a hard surface, turning to crack the entire shell. Do not remove the shell. The cracks will allow the tea to infuse into the egg.

Place the eggs into a pot and fill with enough water to cover by about 2 inches. Add the tea bags, soy sauce, and star anise. Bring to a boil, then turn down heat and simmer for about 30 minutes. Remove from heat and let soak overnight. (Alternatively, make them in a crockpot and cook at low setting for 8 to 10 hours.)

Cool eggs, remove shell, and serve.

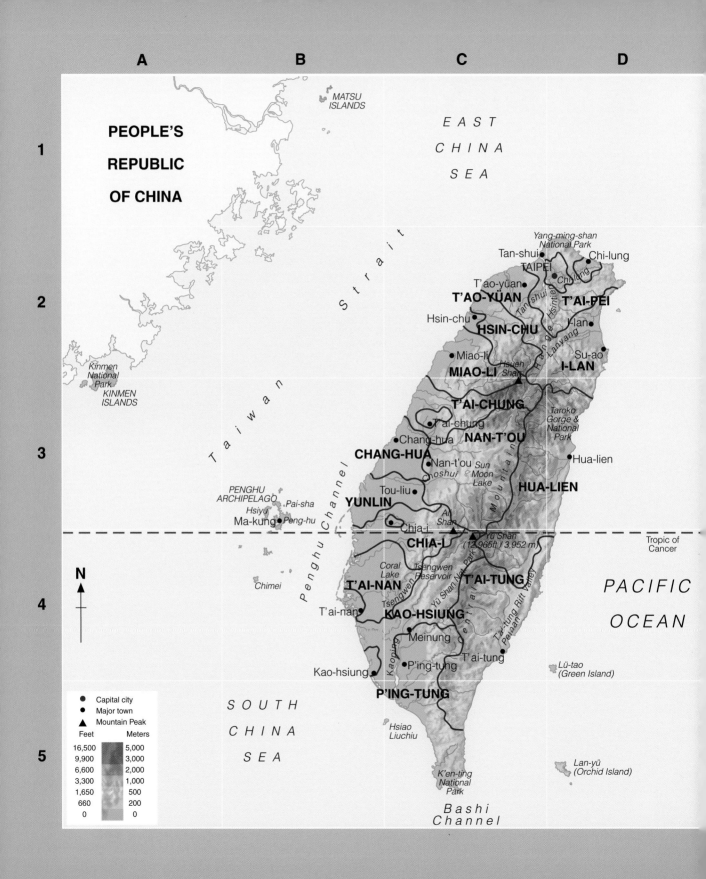

A **B** **C** **D**

1

PEOPLE'S

REPUBLIC

OF CHINA

*MATSU
ISLANDS*

E A S T

C H I N A

S E A

2

*Kinmen
National
Park*

**KINMEN
ISLANDS**

Tan-shui
TAIPEI
T'ao-yüan
T'AO-YÜAN
Hsin-chu
HSIN-CHIU
Miao-li
MIAO-LI

*Yang-ming-shan
National Park*
Chi-lung
Chi-lung
T'AI-PEI
I-lan
Su-ao
I-LAN

*Hsueh
Shan*

T a i w a n

S t r a i t

3

*PENGHU
ARCHIPELAGO*
Pai-sha
Hsiyu *Peng-hu*
Ma-kung● ●Peng-hu

T'AI-CHUNG
T'ai-chung
Chang-hua
NAN-T'OU
CHANG-HUA
Nan-t'ou
Choshui
Tou-liu
YUNLIN

*Taroko
Gorge &
National
Park*
Hua-lien
HUA-LIEN

*Sun
Moon
Lake*

M o u n t a i n s

P e n g h u   C h a n n e l

*Ali
Shan*
Chia-i
CHIA-I

*Yu Shan
(12,965ft) / 3,952 m)*

Tropic of
Cancer

4

N
↑

Chimei

*Coral
Lake*
*Tsengwen
Reservoir*
T'AI-NAN
T'ai-nan
Tsengwen
KAO-HSIUNG
Meinung
Kao-hsiung
Kaoping
P'ing-tung
P'ING-TUNG

Yü Shan Nat Park
T'AI-TUNG
T'ai-tung Rift Valley
Peinan
T'ai-tung

C e n t r a l

PACIFIC

OCEAN

*Lü-tao
(Green Island)*

S O U T H

C H I N A

S E A

*Hsiao
Liuchiu*

*K'en-ting
National
Park*

*Lan-yü
(Orchid Island)*

*B a s h i
C h a n n e l*

5

● Capital city
● Major town
▲ Mountain Peak

Feet		Meters
16,500		5,000
9,900		3,000
6,600		2,000
3,300		1,000
1,650		500
660		200
0		0

MAP OF TAIWAN

ECONOMIC TAIWAN

Services

- ✈ Airport
- ⚛ Nuclear power plant
- 🚢 Port
- 🚂 Railway

Agriculture

- Flowers
- Fruits
- Pig rearing
- Poultry
- Rice
- Tea
- Vegetables

Natural Resources

- Fish

Industry

- Aviation & aerospace
- Biotechnology
- Cement
- Chemicals
- Consumer products
- Electronics
- Iron & steel
- Petroleum refining
- Pharmaceuticals

ABOUT THE ECONOMY

GROSS DOMESTIC PRODUCT (GDP)
$518.8 billion (2015)

GDP PER CAPITA
$47,500 (2015)

GDP BY SECTOR
Agriculture 1.9 percent, industry 34.8 percent, services 63.2 percent (2015)

AGRICULTURAL PRODUCTS
rice, vegetables, fruit, tea, flowers; pigs, poultry; fish

INDUSTRIES
electronics, communications and information technology products, petroleum refining, chemicals, textiles, iron and steel, machinery, cement, food processing, vehicles, consumer products, pharmaceuticals

CURRENCY
Taiwanese Dollar (TWD), symbol NT$ = 100 cents
Notes denominations: NT$1000, 500, 200, 100, 50
Coin denominations: NT$50, 10, 5, 1 USD 1 = TWD 33.33 (February 2016)

POPULATION BELOW POVERTY LINE
1.5 percent (2012)

INFLATION RATE
—0.2 percent (2015)

MAJOR TRADE PARTNERS
China, Hong Kong, United States, Japan, Singapore

TOTAL EXPORTS
$262.6 billion (2015 estimate)

TOTAL IMPORTS
$221.2 billion (2015 estimate)

LABOR FORCE
11.6 million (2015 estimate)

WORKFORCE BY SECTOR
Agriculture 5 percent; industry 36.1 percent; services 58.9 percent (2014)

UNEMPLOYMENT RATE
3.7 percent (2015)

COMMUNICATIONS MEDIA
Telephones: 14 million operating main lines (2014)
Mobile cell phone: 30 million (2014)
Internet hosts: 6.27 million (2012)
Internet users: 18.6 million (2016)

CULTURAL TAIWAN

Formosan Aboriginal Culture Village
The Formosan Aboriginal Culture Village is a showcase of the culture and traditions of Taiwan's indigenous peoples.

Lungshan Temple
One of Taiwan's oldest and most famous temples, it is a striking showcase of temple architecture.

Yang-ming-shan National Park
In this park, visitors can experience the vast variety of nature's creations, such as waterfalls, volcanic craters, lakes, and hot springs.

Chiang Kai-shek Memorial Hall
Taiwan's monument to its late president greets visitors with a Ming-style arch at its main entrance. The Hall is flanked by the National Theater and the National Concert Hall.

Sun Moon Lake
Located at the geographical center of Taiwan, the lake is a picturesque tourist attraction containing emerald waters and surrounded by mountains. The Formosan Aboriginal Culture Village is nearby.

Taipei
The political, cultural, and economic center of Taiwan, Taipei is the largest city of the land.

National Palace Museum
Here, at the National Palace Museum, exhibits of Chinese culture from as far back as the Northern Sung dynasty to the more recent Qing dynasty can be viewed. The museum has one of the most comprehensive collections of Chinese art in the world with more than 700,000 items on display.

Chia-i
The city functions mainly as a departure point from which excursions to the Central Mountain Range can be made. Industrial activity is less concentrated here than in other cities, with most parts of the city centered on manufacturing.

Yü Shan (Jade Mountain)
This is the highest mountain in the Central Ranges.

Matsu Temple at Deer Ear Gate
Almost four hundred years old, this temple is dedicated to the Goddess of the Sea and is also home to the Old Man under the Moon, a Taoist god somewhat like Cupid. Singles who are looking for a spouse pray to this god.

T'ai-nan
The former capital of Taiwan is also its oldest city. T'ai-nan is best known as the cultural and historic center of the island.

The Cave of Eight Immortals
Also known as Pahsien Tung (PAH-Hsien Tung) in Chinese, there are actually fourteen caves located in this area. It has been designated as a site of national archaeological importance due to the discovery of numerous artifacts.

ABOUT THE CULTURE

OFFICIAL NAME
Republic of China

CAPITAL
Taipei

NATIONAL FLAG
Red with a white sun on a blue rectangle in the upper left hand corner. The blue, white, and red colors represent the Three Principles of the People set out by Sun Yat-sen.

NATIONAL ANTHEM
The National Anthem of the Republic of China, often called the "San Min Chu I" (SAN Min JOO Ee), or the "Three Principles of the People." The anthem is banned on mainland China.

NATIONAL FLOWER
Prunus mei (plum blossom)

HIGHEST POINT
Yü Shan (12,965 feet or 3,952 m)

MAJOR RIVERS
Kaoping, Choshui, Tan-shui

MAJOR LAKES
Tsengwen Reservoir, Coral Lake, Sun Moon Lake

MAJOR CITIES
Taipei, Kao-hsiung, T'ai-chung, T'ai-nan

ADMINISTRATIVE DIVISIONS
Counties: Chang-hua, Chia-i, Hsin-chu, Hua-lien, I-lan, Kao-hsiung, Kinmen, Lien-chiang, Miao-li, Nan-t'ou, Peng-hu, Ping-tung, T'ai-chung, T'ai-nan, T'ai-pei, T'ai-tung, T'ao-yüan, Yun-lin
Municipalities: Chia-i, Hsin-chu, Chi-lung, T'ai-chung, T'ai-nan
Special municipalities: Kaohsiung City, Taipei City

POPULATION
23,415,126 (July 2015 estimate)

LIFE EXPECTANCY
79.98 years (2015)

ETHNIC GROUPS
Taiwanese (including Hakka) 84 percent, mainland Chinese 14 percent, aborigines 2 percent.

RELIGIOUS GROUPS
Mixture of Buddhist, Confucian, and Taoist 93 percent, Christian 4.5 percent, other 2.5 percent.

LANGUAGES
Mandarin Chinese (official), Taiwanese (minority), Hakka dialects

TIMELINE

IN TAIWAN	IN THE WORLD
	753 BCE Rome is founded.
	116–117 CE The Roman Empire reaches its greatest extent, under Emperor Trajan.
600 CE Island is occupied by aboriginal community of Austronesian descent.	**600 CE** Height of Mayan civilization
	1000 The Chinese perfect gunpowder and begin to use it in warfare.
1517 Island is sighted by Portuguese vessels en route to Japan and named *Ilha Formosa* (Beautiful Island).	**1530** Beginning of transatlantic slave trade organized by the Portuguese in Africa.
	1558–1603 Reign of Elizabeth I of England
	1620 Pilgrims sail the *Mayflower* to America.
1624 Dutch occupy and control Formosa.	
1662 Dutch are defeated by Chinese Ming general Cheng Cheng Kung (Koxinga) whose family rules Formosa for a short period.	
1683 Annexed by China's rulers the Manchu Qing.	**1776** US Declaration of Independence
	1789–1799 The French Revolution
	1861 The US Civil War begins.
	1869 The Suez Canal is opened.
1895 Ceded "in perpetuity" to Japan under the Treaty of Shimonoseki at the end of the Sino-Japanese war.	
1911 China becomes the Republic of China.	**1914–1918** World War I.
	1939–1945 World War II.

IN TAIWAN	IN THE WORLD
1945	
Taiwan recovered by China's Nationalist Kuomintang government.	
1949	**1949**
Flight of Nationalist government to Taiwan after Chinese Communist revolution. China becomes the People's Republic of China.	The North Atlantic Treaty Organization (NATO) is formed.
1954	
United States–Taiwanese mutual defense treaty is signed.	**1957**
	The Russians launch *Sputnik 1*.
	1966–1969
	The Chinese Cultural Revolution
1971	
Taiwan withdraws from the UN.	
1986	**1986**
Democratic Progressive Party (DPP) is formed as an opposition to nationalist Kuomintang (KMT).	Nuclear power disaster at Chernobyl in Ukraine
	1991
	Breakup of the Soviet Union
	1997
2000	Hong Kong is returned to China.
Proindependence candidate, Chen Shui-bian, is elected president of Taiwan.	
2001	**2001**
Taiwan partially lifts its fifty-two-year ban on direct trade and communications with China.	Terrorists crash planes in New York, Washington, DC, and Pennsylvania.
2002	
Taiwan becomes a member of the WTO.	**2003**
2004	War in Iraq
Chen Shui-bian is reelected as president of Taiwan; country's first national referendum.	
2005	
National Assembly elected.	**2008**
	United States elects first African-American president, Barack Obama.
2016	**2016**
Earthquake February 6 causes 117 deaths in Tainan.	Islamist terrorists attack Brussels.
In May, Tsai Ing-wen becomes first woman president of Taiwan.	

GLOSSARY

cha (cha)
Tea, the national drink of Taiwan.

changshan (CHAHNG shan)
Traditional costume for men.

cheongsam (CHEE-ong sahm)
Traditional costume for women.

Confucianism
A code of conduct or value system that is a fundamental pillar of Chinese culture.

dim sum (DIM sum)
Cantonese-style snacks that are served with tea in Taiwan's tea houses. They are also known as yum cha (YAHM chah).

fan (fahn)
Rice, the staple food in Taiwan.

feng shui (FEHNG shway)
Literally meaning "wind and water," this oriental art of geomancy is based on the belief that nonliving objects can influence people's living environment.

Han (Hahn)
The name given to the Chinese people who are believed to have originated from the central plains of China. Today the Han Chinese are the dominant ethnic group of China.

hongbao (HOHNG bow)
Traditional red envelope gifts of money.

hsiao (SEE-ow)
The Confucian virtue of filial piety or respect and obedience to family elders.

kan pei (GAHN bay)
Literally meaning "bottoms up," it is like saying "cheers" during a toast.

Kuo yu (GWOH ewe-ee)
The national language, or Mandarin.

martial law
The suspension of ordinary law, invoked by a government in an emergency, with the military taking control instead

pinyin (PIN-yin)
The Romanization system for the Chinese language.

shan (shahn)
Mountain.

tai chi chuan (TAI jee CHWAHN)
Also called tai chi, the Chinese art of shadow-boxing with meditative movements that is a popular leisure activity and form of exercise in Taiwan.

tai fong (TAI fohng)
Typhoon, or a tropical cyclone that commonly occurs in parts of Northeast Asia, especially in Taiwan, Hong Kong, and southern China.

yuan (YOO-ahn)
Meaning "council." Taiwan's five yuan make up the national government, together with the president and National Assembly.

FOR FURTHER INFORMATION

BOOKS

Erway, Cathy. *The Food of Taiwan: Recipes from the Beautiful Island*. New York: Houghton Mifflin Harcourt Publishing, 2015.

Kelly, Robert, and Chung Wah Chow. *Lonely Planet: Taiwan*. London: Lonely Planet Publications, 9th edition, 2014.

Li-Hung, Hsiao. Translated by Michelle Wu. *A Thousand Moons on a Thousand Rivers*. New York: Columbia University Press, 2001 (originally published in Taiwan in 1980).

Lin, Hsiao-ting. *Accidental State: Chiang Kai-shek, the United States, and the Making of Taiwan*. Cambridge, MA: Harvard University Press, 2016.

Lu, Hsiu-lien. *My Fight for a New Taiwan: One Woman's Journey from Prison to Power*. Seattle: University of Washington Press, 2016.

Macdonald, Phil. *National Geographic Traveler: Taiwan*, 3rd edition. Washington, DC: National Geographic, 2011.

FILMS

City of Sadness. Directed by Hou Hsiao-hsien. 3-H Films, 1989.

Crouching Tiger, Hidden Dragon. Directed by Ang Lee. Sony Pictures Entertainment Inc., 2000.

Eat Drink Man Woman. Directed by Ang Lee. Samuel Goldwyn Company, 1994.

The Wedding Banquet. Directed by Ang Lee. Samuel Goldwyn Company, 1993.

ONLINE

BBC News. Taiwan country Profile. www.bbc.com/news/world-asia-16164639

CIA World Factbook, Taiwan. www.cia.gov/library/publications/the-world-factbook/geos/tw.html

Lonely Planet, Taiwan. www.lonelyplanet.com/taiwan

The *New York Times*, Times Topics: Taiwan. topics.nytimes.com/top/news/international/countriesandterritories/taiwan/index.html

Republic of China. www.taiwan.gov.tw

Taipei Times. www.taipeitimes.com

Taiwan. eng.taiwan.net.tw

BIBLIOGRAPHY

BBC News. Taiwan country Profile. http://www.bbc.com/news/world-asia-16164639.

CIA World Factbook, Taiwan. https://www.cia.gov/library/publications/the-world-factbook/geos/tw.html.

Cole, J. Michael. "Taiwan's Aboriginal Culture Threatened by China." *The Diplomat*, August 8, 2014. http://thediplomat.com/2014/08/taiwans-aboriginal-culture-threatened-by-china.

Consonery, Nicholas. "What Taiwan's Elections Mean for China's Economic Future." *Fortune*, January 19, 2016. http://fortune.com/2016/01/19/taiwan-tsai-ing-wen-china.

Dou, Eva, and Jenny H. Hsu. "How Convenient: In Taiwan, the 24/7 Store Does It All." *The Wall Street Journal*, May 16, 2014. http://www.wsj.com/articles/SB1000142405270230451870457952037124390368O.

The *Economist*. "Straightened Circumstances." November 14, 2015. http://www.economist.com/news/finance-and-economics/21678276-weaker-growth-exposes-downside-ties-china-straitened-circumstances.

Jennings, Ralph. "Leopards found extinct in Taiwan as public begins to growl." *The Christian Science Monitor*, May 6, 2013. http://www.csmonitor.com/World/Global-News/2013/0506/Leopards-found-extinct-in-Taiwan-as-public-begins-to-growl.

Lai, Alex. "Prison Break: Ju Ming at the Hong Kong Museum of Art." Sotheby's, March 17, 2014. www.sothebys.com/en/news-video/blogs/all-blogs/eye-on-asia/2014/03/prison-break-ju-ming-hong-kong-museum-of-art.html.

The *New York Times*, Times Topics: Taiwan. http://topics.nytimes.com/top/news/international/countriesandterritories/taiwan/index.html.

Nylander, Johan. "Strong Support for Independence in Taiwan." *Forbes*, Feb. 14, 2015. http://www.forbes.com/sites/jnylander/2015/02/14/strong-support-for-independence-in-taiwan/#77d21dc26f8f.

Taipei Times. http://www.taipeitimes.com.

INDEX

INDEX